I0868128

Beaumetz-lès-Cambrai War Cemetery No. 1, Pas-de-Calais, WW1 (architect: Wilfred Clement von Berg)

# NEVER AGAIN
## GARDENS OF PEACE

### A LANDSCAPE AND ARCHITECTURAL HISTORY OF WAR CEMETERIES

Edited by Michel Racine

Marie-Madeleine Damien
Paul Gough
Bernard Klein
Isabelle Loodts
Chantal Pradines
Simon Rietz

Photographs by Christine Bastin & Jacques Evrard

Mercatorfonds
Distributed outside Belgium,
Luxemburg and the Netherlands
by Yale University Press

British 'Two Tree War Cemetery', Ayette, Moyenneville, Pas-de-Calais, WW1 (architect: William Harrison Cowlishaw)

Soupir German War Cemetery, Aisne, WW1 (architect: Robert Tischler)

# INTRODUCTION

*'Le cimetière est un jardin à part entière'.*

ALAIN HERVÉ[1]

## Stones of memory, soil of solace, landscapes of consciousness

The beauty of the numerous war and memorial cemeteries created to honour the fallen of the First World War and the many conflicts that ensued truly stuns visitors. Designed with sensitive attention to the surrounding battle landscapes, their smallest details were also treated meticulously, in accordance with the rules of each nation. Each belligerent country developed its specific identity, its recognisable style and its own approach to war and the memory of its dead. Most of these cemeteries are true gardens, maintained impeccably by teams of professionals, and offering moments of intense emotion, introspection and awareness ... as so many manifestations of remembrance and peace demonstrate: 'Peaceful and beautiful! Moving, emotional +. *Merci!* Immaculately kept. *Je remercie les soldats pour la paix.* We owe you so much. *Merci pour notre liberté. Nie wieder Krieg!* We remember, thank you! *Würdig! Lieu sublime!* Thank you for such a peaceful resting place for my great-uncle! *Belles sépultures, merci. Magnifique cimetière.* Beautiful and tranquil. *Pèlerinage émouvant!* Beautiful place! *Magnifique hommage à nos soldats!* So peaceful! *Très beau! Prachtig! Zo goed onderhouden!* Very moving experience! *Schön gehalten!* Beautifully kept! Very touching! Peaceful, moving and beautifully kept. A very poignant resting place! Thank you for maintaining it!'[2]

Geoff Dyer, one of the writers who has best described the terrible battles of the First World War, recalls his own experience when he discovered Redan Ridge Cemetery No. 1, a small burial ground on the front line in Beaumont-Hamel: 'one of the most beautiful places on earth [...] Standing here, I know that some part of me will always be calmed by the memory of this place, by the vast capacity for forgiveness revealed by these cemeteries, by this landscape.'[3] As in so many other war cemeteries, a dual sensation surfaces at the end of an empty path running through the fields. On the one hand, an emotion provoked by the sublime character of a perfect geometry set in the undulations of the landscape, the care given to the composition, the small-scale architecture, planting, the slightest details; on the other, the satisfaction of progressively discovering, moving from one grave to the next, a perfection that comes together with ethics, the equal treatment of the men who died in battle, the attribution of an individual grave to each of the identified bodies, the simplicity of the inscription on the identical headstones, devoid of class distinction, and respect for the various faiths. Countless memorials with the same characteristics give the families of the fallen and humanity as a whole a place to reflect. If it is true that, as Max Jacob stated, 'Everything that exists is situated', the living need a place – monument or garden – where they can find the names of their missing and their dead, to locate them somewhere in their thoughts.[4] Artistic emotion and consciousness of the horrors of war merge into one another in these gardens on the battlefields, thus contradicting Jacob's words: 'I am convinced that artistic emotion ceases when analysis and thought intervene: causing people to reflect and giving them an experience of beauty are two very different things'.[5] One only needs to visit a few war cemeteries of either world wars to see this: the experience of beauty endlessly blends with remembrance, assuaging the darkest thoughts, while the dialogue with the landscape rings loudly: 'Jamais plus! Never again! Nie wieder!'

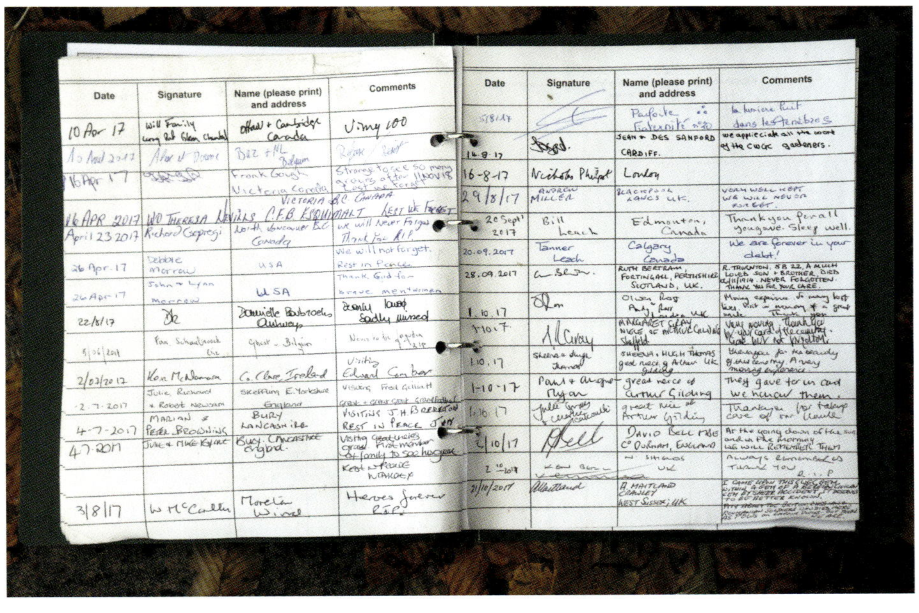

*Visitor's Book*, La Neuville British Cemetery, Corbie, Somme, 2019

Visitors give their thanks. But beauty does not fall from the heavens. Each of the works of art raises questions: created on territory ceded by France, each seemingly speaks of the country of origin of the soldiers, while at the same time making peace with the landscape of the living, where it is inscribed for eternity. As we visit these cemeteries, we inevitably compare the way in which each country buried and honoured its fallen who had died far away from home. We see that many of these cemeteries and memorials reflect various garden and landscape cultures, and that many deserve to be recognised as examples of consciousness heritage in addition to that of their architecture and landscape gardening. As we embark on this vast undertaking we want to simultaneously focus on a selection of outstanding works that represent the various cultures and help our readers to understand these gardens of peace by shedding light on their origins in garden history. They can indeed be situated within the evolution of the landscape of the dead in the western world – from 'death enters the garden' in English landscaped gardens;[6] to the 'revolution of cemeteries' in late eighteenth-century Europe;[7] right up to the invention of war cemeteries and memorials to the missing during the industrial warfare of the nineteenth and twentieth centuries.

The governments of the various countries engaged in the First World War rapidly found themselves in unimaginable conditions, as they confronted the urgent needs imposed by the situation. They had to integrate multicultural and multifaith dimensions, bury hundreds and then millions of bodies that came from all directions, all the while responding to the demands of the families – impossible to satisfy on this scale – to return their relatives' bodies ... For centuries, with the rare exception of some officers, fallen soldiers had ended up in mass graves. However, by the First World War, times had changed. After the spread of ideas of the Enlightenment (the Lumières; the Aufklärung) – on equality, human rights, freedom of thought, tolerance and universalism, and moreover the relationship between Church and State, and notions about the afterlife – burial conditions and the design of graveyards had evolved in all the countries engaged in the conflict. A decent burial was now a right, regardless of social class. This 'novelty of the revolutionary era', founded on France's Imperial Decree on Burials of 12 June 1804, restored the cult of the dead and established the right of each person to a headstone, an emblem of remembrance.[8] The memorial projects of the architects of Revolutionary France and the invention of a new landscape of the dead at Paris's Père Lachaise Cemetery in 1804 had a considerable influence on burial rites and architecture throughout the nineteenth century, particularly in the United States, England and Germany. Responding to these increasingly shared aspirations, brand new designs and ways of managing cemeteries saw the light of day, ranging from landscaping to private management: the rural cemeteries in the United States and the nondenominational cemeteries in England. The architectures and landscape designs of these civilian cemeteries reflected new common values: the Egyptian Revival style was adopted for monumental portals and headstones, breaking away from the Gothic Revival style that had been so dear to the Church; a freedom within the general visual composition was reaffirmed, with sinuous paths making their way through meadows, alongside streams and groves made up of new species of trees.

The dignified burial of soldiers had begun during the large-scale wars of the second half of the nineteenth century, whose scope and size inaugurated the mass carnage of so-called modern warfare. In 1862, during the American Civil War, Congress decided to bury the Union soldiers in individual graves. Virginia's Arlington National Cemetery was inaugurated two years later. During the Second Boer War (1899–1902), the British Empire showed its respect for its citizens who had died in South Africa, giving them individual graves and erecting memorials into which the names of the deceased were inscribed.

During the First World War and in the years that followed, the authorities of each country were faced with dealing with appalling masses of victims, who had often been hastily buried in makeshift burial grounds. The legitimate expectations of the families and populations had to be considered, sites had to be found where multiple cemeteries could be created, burial methods had to be determined and a landscaping approach had to be defined. Infused by the spirit of the Enlightenment and a secular culture of garden art, the British played a pioneering role in the middle of the First World War when they created the Imperial War Graves Commission (IWGC), simultaneously inventing the war cemetery landscaped like a garden and the remembrance memorial, a monumental creation that would – in some way – compensate for an absence of bodies. This creative impetus blended modernist and neoclassical influences, and was to continue before and after the Second World War. The Volksbund Deutsche Kriegsgräberfürsorge (VDK), the German counterpart to the IWGC, had been created in 1919; for some time its mostly unknown realisations were marked by the National Socialist aesthetic.

Even today, though, oblivion still hovers over the countless civilian victims of war. Counting from the beginning of the First World War, their number is higher than that of dead soldiers. With its 35 million civilian victims in comparison with 30 million dead military, the Second World War marked a chilling turning point. Most often, civilians were buried individually by their families and friends. But until today, apart from a few exceptions, the authorities have not yet addressed this vital duty of remembrance.

The images captured by Christine Bastin and Jacques Evrard confirm the comments found in visitors' books and registers, and indeed delve deeper. These professional photographers, known for exploring unfamiliar landscapes and architecture, walked through former battlefields, from Belgium to Alsace and Normandy, and with great sensitivity make evident the richness of this cultural heritage. They did not limit themselves to a few sites or the well-documented British War Cemeteries, but also photographed many of the German burial grounds as well as those of the United States and other countries.[9] Following in their footsteps, we discover hundreds of unknown cemeteries and memorials. They take us on a walk that invites us to compare the belligerents' different approaches to the burial of the dead and to find out more about the how these landscaped cemeteries reflect the different landscape, garden and architecture cultures of the various countries.

The rambles and research of Christine and Jacques converge with my own, and our studies have fed one another over many years. Having discovered the gardens of northern and eastern France[10] and completed a study of garden tourism in the Nord region,[11] I included some war cemeteries in the selection of gardens that were included in my guides to French gardens. In this context, I also organised a seminar for garden owners entitled 'Jardins de Picardie' at the Historial of the Great War in Péronne.[12] In 2007, during the training of future landscape gardeners at the École Nationale Supérieure de Paysage of Versailles, we asked the students to compare the landscape designs of the British, German and French war cemeteries with Pascal Cribier's minimalist approach for remembrance at the Donjon de Vez garden.[13] A special issue of the international architecture magazine *Casabella* devoted to memorials and its superb photographs of Sir Edwin Lutyens's tower and cross at Villers-Bretonneux (Somme) encouraged me to pursue the discovery of these lessons for landscape design and architecture.[14] We found that we were not alone in thinking that along the roads of the Western Front and of Normandy, just like everywhere in the world, there were unknown magnificent gardens like those that we had started documenting in the early 1980s.[15]

Through their shared origins with the art of gardens, many of these war cemeteries and memorials refer back to previous remarkable and significant creations. Although a more obscure part of the art movements of the interwar era, the creation of these places necessitated the participation of exceptional architects, landscape architects, gardeners and artists. There is no doubt that this wonderful landscape and architectural heritage deserves an international inventory, a work of remembrance that will allow it to be recognised as a shared heritage of a common consciousness. **M.R.**

---

1 'The cemetery is a fully developed garden': Alain Hervé interviewed by Michel Racine in 2002. Hervé (1932–2019) was founder of the French branch of Friends of the Earth (founded in 1970) and editor-in-chief of *Le Sauvage* magazine (founded in 1973).

2 Comments drawn from registers and visitors' books.

3 Geoff Dyer, *The Missing of the Somme* (London: Canongate), 1994, p. 130.

4 Max Jacob, preface to *Cornet à dés* (1916), in *The Dice Cup*, trans. Christopher Pilling and David Kennedy (London: Atlas Press), 2000, p. 13.

5 Ibid., p. 15.

6 Michel Baridon, *Cours sur les jardins anglais*, École Nationale Supérieure de Paysage Versailles, 2007.

7 Michel Vovelle and Régis Bertrand, *La Ville des morts: Essai sur l'imaginaire urbain contemporain d'après les cimetières provençaux* (Paris: Éditions du CNRS), 1983.

8 *Guide du cimetière du Père-Lachaise* of 1836, quoted in Philippe Ariès, *L'homme devant la mort* (Paris: Éditions du Seuil), 1977, vol. 2, p. 226.

9 Studies of British cemeteries include Jeroen Geurst, *Cemeteries of the Great War by Sir Edwin Lutyens* (Rotterdam: 010 Publishers), 2010; and Frank Rambert, *Jardins de guerre: Les cimetières britanniques sur le front ouest* (Geneva: MetisPresses), 2014.

10 While preparing our guides to gardens: Michel Racine, *Le Guide des jardins de France; Jardins en France* (Arles: Actes Sud), 2004 (and previous editions); *Guide des jardins en France* (Paris: Ulmer), 2 vols, 2007.

11 Michel Racine, *Pour une politique des jardins et paysages d'intérêt culturel en région Nord-Pas-de-Calais*, intro. Philippe Nys, Préfecture de Région Nord-Pas-de-Calais/Délégation Régionale au Tourisme, Association XIX-20, ARPEJ, 1995.

12 'Jardins de Picardie', day training courses (Institut régional de Picardie), Historial de la Grande Guerre, Péronne, 14 and 15 October 1997.

13 Donjon de Vez, Oise, northern France. Garden created by Pascal Cribier and Patrick Ecoutin in 1989.

14 Sissi Castellano, 'Sir Edwin Lutyens e i cimiteri della Grande Guerra nel nord della Francia', *Casabella* 675 (February 2000), pp. 6–27.

15 The first inventory of French gardens (a Mission Paysage initiative) was Michel Racine, Ernest Boursier-Mougenot and Françoise Binet, *Inventaire des jardins d'intérêt historique, paysager et botanique de la région Provence-Alpes-Côte d'Azur*, 1980.

Thiepval Anglo-French Memorial to the Missing, Somme, WW1 (architect: Edwin Lutyens)

## From respect for the fallen, to their disintegration in the landscape

For many centuries the bodies of the dead combatants of European and western wars were buried near the battlefields. This method of burial was determined by the contingencies of the situation and the funeral practices of the social groups that took charge of the bodies – and often the souls, according to whether there was a belief, or not, in an afterlife. From antiquity right up to the twentieth century, the obligation to bury the bodies – sometimes the ashes – of soldiers on the battlefield, or nearby, remained a constant element that became increasingly imperative with the mass wars of the nineteenth and twentieth centuries.

In Athens in the fifth century BCE, headstones bearing the names of citizens killed in combat and organised into their tribes testified to the resolve to keep the memory of the dead alive, to pay homage and memorialise the tragic event. This was a way of mourning the dead both individually and collectively, at the same time as celebrating war. In 339 BCE, after the Battle of Chaeronea and the victory of Philip II of Macedonia over Athens and its allies, both camps buried their dead according to their religious rites in order to ward off the wrath of the gods. The Thebans erected a monument topped with a stone lion on the mound where their dead were laid to rest.[1] Attaching huge importance to the passage of the dead to another life, the Romans took great care in their cremation and burial rites, except for slaves who were unceremoniously thrown into communal graves. Legionaries were either buried at the foots of headstones, such as those found across the former Roman Empire, or were buried in communal graves after the great battles. Under a decision made by the Roman General Germanicus in 15 CE, the reburial of the remains of legionaries (killed six years previously during the Battle of the Teutoburg Forest against Germanic tribes) is evidence of a particularly sophisticated civilisation that showed immense respect for its soldiers and a duty to ease their transition to the afterlife.[2]

However, during the countless wars that tore Europe apart for centuries, spanning the fall of the Roman Empire to the First World War, and including the Seven Years War, frequent religious wars and Napoleonic conflicts, few families could afford burial places for soldiers killed on the battlefields. The burial place for fallen soldiers almost always remained the common grave, a landscape for immediate oblivion that resulted in the definitive loss of identity, regardless of rank or nationality. Sometimes, the absence of graves meant that dead soldiers were at the mercy of birds and wild animals, before disappearing into the landscape, their bodies dissolving into the ground. Each was doomed to 'wander like a lost soul'.[3] Before visiting Waterloo – 'this lonely and funereal plateau, / This sinister field where God fused so much annihilation'[4] – Victor Hugo described, with infinite accuracy, the landscape swallowing up the corpses:

> Waterloo! Waterloo! Waterloo!
> Dismal plain!
> Like a wave of water which bubbles over
> in an overfilled urn,
> Within your circle of forests,
> hills, valleys,
> Pale death mingles among
> the melancholic battalions.[5]

Following these practices during the Napoleonic Wars, which ignored the multitude of fallen soldiers, it was not until the American Civil War (1861–5) – the first mass war of the nineteenth century – that military cemeteries, as they became widespread during the First World War, started to emerge. In the meantime, burial procedures for civilians in Europe and the United States had developed slowly, through the rebirth of a cult of the dead in eighteenth-century gardens, the 'revolution of cemeteries' and the recognition of 'the right to be buried regardless of race or religion'.[6] **M.R.**

---

1 In 1880, 226 skeletons were unearthed at the site. See Yves Le Maner, 'L'histoire des sépultures militaires de l'Antiquité au XIXe siècle', *Chemins de Mémoire 14–18*, Centre d'Histoire et de Mémoire du Nord–Pas-de-Calais <www.cheminsdememoire-nordpasdecalais.fr/lhistoire/la-memoire-de-la-grande-guerre/lhistoire-des-sepultures-militaires-de-lantiquite-au-xixe-siecle>.

2 Ibid.

3 'And as for our dead, if all their souls feel troubled, / It's not because they can't die of love, good heavens, no, / But because they can't get themselves slain next time. / Each of them dreams of having his name on a war memorial.' *(Quant à nos trépassés, s'ils ont tous l'âme en peine, / C'est pas d'être hors d'état d'mourir d'amour, cré nom de nom, / Mais de ne plus pouvoir se faire occire à la prochaine. / Au monument aux morts, chacun rêve d'avoir son nom.)* Georges Brassens, 'Les Patriotes', from the album *Trompe-la-mort* (1976).

4 *'Waterloo, ce plateau funèbre et solitaire, / Ce champ sinistre où Dieu mêla tant de néants'*. From Victor Hugo, 'L'expiation (II)', in *Les Châtiments*, Paris, 1853.

5 *'Waterloo! Waterloo! Waterloo! morne plaine! / Comme une onde qui bout dans une urne trop pleine, / Dans ton cirque de bois, de coteaux, de vallons, / La pâle mort mêlait les sombres bataillons.'* Ibid.

6 For the rebirth of a cult of the dead, see Michel Vovelle and Régis Bertrand, *La Ville des morts: Essai sur l'imaginaire urbain contemporain d'après les cimetières provençaux* (Paris: Éditions du CNRS), 1983.

Lion's Mound, 1826, plain of Waterloo, Belgium

Headstones for Roman legionaries of the Eighth Legion of Augustus, circa late 1st and early 2nd centuries. Discovered in the Koenigshoffen district of Strasbourg, during archaeological excavations carried out by ANTEA-Archéologie in 2018.

# FROM CEMETERY TO GARDEN

### *Ad sanctos* burials: graveyards around church towers and interments inside churches

Cemeteries as we know them today are only two centuries old. The invention of military cemeteries goes back to the American Civil War and the First World War. The intermingled origins of both deserve to be better known, particularly if we are to look at the history of gardens that characterises each country. Our emotion when experiencing the landscape of military cemeteries comes from far back in time, fed by the evolution of ideas about the afterlife and the burial or cremation methods specific to civilians and soldiers.

In the Gallo-Roman culture, the world of the dead was clearly separated from the world of the living. Cremation was the most common practice. Ashes were collected in an urn that was then buried in the family plot or beneath a headstone bearing an epitaph. With the growth of Christianity around 300 CE, cremation vanished and the dead were buried. It seems that during the Middle Ages, burials within a perimeter protected by the right of asylum around places of worship coexisted with inhumations scattered around dwellings.[1] From the consecration of cemeteries in the tenth century until the French Revolution, the place reserved for dead civilians in Europe progressed along with changes in the perception of death and the afterlife. Encouraged by the Church, people were buried under places of worship or in consecrated cemeteries. Jews, suicide victims, heretics and unbaptised children were excluded from these cemeteries and had to be interred outside the city walls. Monks had the great privilege of being buried in the orchard gardens of their monastic compounds, as is shown in the well-known ninth-century plan of the Benedictine Abbey of St Gall, in Switzerland. But for ordinary people, 'no Christian dead in the community of the faithful may be buried elsewhere than in a church or blessed cemetery'.[2] These were *ad sanctos* burials, close to the tombs of saints, in cemeteries surrounding the churches.[3] The wealthier were buried in the building itself, as close as possible to the altar containing the relics of saints, which were vested with the authority of interceding with God to shorten the time spent in Purgatory before going to Heaven. Gradually, the floors of churches became covered in slabs under which the corpses of the rich families were stacked,[4] while the less wealthy were interred in the adjoining cemetery and the poor were thrown in the communal grave.

Although the cemetery was generally a piece of vacant land, where individual identity disappeared, funerary ideas and practices evolved in the mid-eighteenth century. Churches were filled with decomposing cadavers whose smell was deemed toxic according to miasma theory, where 'bad air' played a fundamental role in the spread of infections and epidemics. The 'toxic vapours' were condemned by those concerned, including doctors and members of the clergy, such as some bishops and Abbot Charles-Gabriel Porée, author of *Lettres sur la sépulture dans les églises*, a study that had a real impact in France.[5] The question of public health became increasingly decisive in the evolution of ideas about burial practices when, with the acceleration of European demographic growth, cemeteries overflowed with corpses and the material impossibility of keeping them inside the city walls progressively became an obvious fact and a political challenge. **M.R.**

The marble floor of St John's Co-Cathedral in Valletta, Malta, is composed of a series of tombs, housing about 400 members of The Order of Knights of the Hospital of Saint John of Jerusalem, early 17th–late 18th century.

1 See Elisabeth Zadora-Rio, 'Lieux d'inhumation et espaces consacrés: Le voyage du pape Urbain II en France (août 1095–août 1096)', in André Vauchez (ed.), *Lieux sacrés, Lieux de culte, Sanctuaires: Approches terminologiques, méthodologiques, historiques et monographiques* (Rome: École française de Rome), 2000, pp. 197–213.

2 Pope Paul V's *Rituale Romanum* (*Roman Ritual*) of 1614.

3 The Greek origin of the word 'cemetery' (*koimētērion*) refers to a place of sleep, evoking the eternal sleep of the dead.

4 'This practice is more or less generalised in southern Europe, while Protestant regions seem to have suffered a lesser invasion of places of worship'; see Régis Bertrand and Anne Carol (eds), *Aux origines des cimetières contemporains: Les réformes funéraires de l'Europe occidentale, XVIIIe–XIXe siècle* (Aix-en-Provence: Presses universitaires de Provence), 2016.

5 Abbé Charles-Gabriel Porée, *Lettres sur la sépulture dans les églises*, Paris, 1749, quoted in Bertrand and Carol, op. cit.

### When death enters the garden

In the eighteenth century, at a time when burials inside a church or in adjoining churchyards often proved impossible for practical reasons, an important intellectual, philosophical and scientific movement was flourishing in Europe. Known as the Enlightenment in England ('Lumières' in France and 'Aufklärung' in Germany), this pushed forward beliefs about the afterlife, and consequently about burial methods and places. New values pervaded, often disseminated by the Freemasons in England, and by discussions between its most influential members – who included intellectuals, politicians, artists and architects – and the European intelligentsia. These ideals were based on rationalism, experimentation, tolerance, the respect of individual liberties and a harmonious relationship between man and nature. In the field of landscape design, the celebration of such a close relationship refers to painting as the desirable model for the arrangement of gardens, but with the integration of death as a major element. This innovation first emerged in the landscaped gardens of England and in Freemasonry circles, where death was a central point of the initiation. In 1726 in Castle Howard, chronicles of cemeteries in Europe came together with the history of gardens when Charles Howard and architect John Vanbrugh discussed building a family mausoleum inside the estate. It was to be placed on a terrace overlooking the landscape and be the same height as the house. One would simply have to walk across a field to reach it. The edifice was designed and built by Nicholas Hawksmoor between 1729 and 1736, after Vanbrugh's death. With its circular plan and Doric columns, the mausoleum was inspired by an engraving by Pietro Santi Bartoli representing the tomb of Roman Emperor Gallienus on the Via Appia. While introducing the concept of death into the landscape, the mausoleum also affirmed a sceptical attitude towards religion, all the time avoiding entombment in a church. The beauty of the building standing on its mound recalls the famous words of English writer Horace Walpole: 'a mausoleum that would tempt one to be buried alive'.[1]

The idea was topical. In 1735, poet Alexander Pope erected a monument of filial piety in memory of his mother on his small Twickenham estate created in 1719. The idea behind the memorial obelisk was that 'all gardening is landscape painting. Just like a landscape hung up'.[2] In England's landscaped gardens, then all across Europe, Masonic references to geometry, the 'Great Architect of the Universe' and Egypt thrived, following the idea that Euclid's teachings on the fundamental evolution of craftsmanship and masonry took place after the Flood. Such references found their place in all the arts, particularly in gardens, through the symbolic plays on the shapes placed in the landscape.[3] More than all other art forms, architecture is at the heart of the Mason's thoughts, where it is in a dialectic relationship with morality. It was the importance attributed to Vitruvius's architecture during the Italian Renaissance, to Andrea Palladio and his Villa La Rotonda, but also to Egypt and its emblematic structures – pyramids, sphinxes, obelisks, etc. – that were the inspirations for 'eye-catchers' and invitations to initiatory journeys: the obelisk at Castle Howard, the pyramid and The Temple of British Worthies at Stowe House, the obelisks at Rousham House and at Stourhead, the Needle's Eye at Wentworth, the obelisk at Claremont House, the temple at Chiswick House ...[4] New values were articulated along a coded journey, within a nature designed to be like theatre.[5]

As both spectator and initiated actor, the stroller is invited to take part in the creator's intentions for the new landscape, sharing *in situ* the reveries of a journey through an idealised Rome and villas of the Italian Renaissance. Moreover, walkers are invited to meditate on death. Displaying a genuine fascination for death, various tombstones, urns and other monuments pace the course of visitors, who are invited to associate a grove, a hill, a pond, a tree or a path with the memory of a lady or gentleman,[6] a family member, or even a pet animal. The most revealing and thought-provoking of the follies in the garden of Rousham House, a grotto, bears the inscription 'In Front of this Stone lie the Remains of Ringwood an Otter-hound of extraordinary Sagacity', showing the owner's dream of Arcadia where his hunting companion has a place of honour.[7]

This new way of thinking about, creating and experiencing the garden spread across Europe in varying interpretations that related to the cross-fertilisation between the movements of ideas of each country and the specific characteristics of their landscapes. In France this development emerged around 1730 but it wasn't until the last third of the century that it appeared in the form of the landscaped garden.[8] In 1771 – incorporating existing picturesque elements, such as sheep pens, floating bridges, wooden footbridges and even a windmill that was already part of the scenery – Claude-Henri Watelet, regular visitor at court and amateur artist, designed the Moulin Joly park on an island in the river Seine. The park quickly became famous and was visited by high society. Marie Antoinette is said to have gone there on several occasions. 'Here is the image of joyful days', exclaimed Watelet, who published his *Essai sur les jardins* in 1774. He defined the 'basic notion of the new parks: picturesque, poetic, Romanesque'. For this painter and engraver, the 'poetic is borrowed from the Egyptian and Greek mythologies' in scenes that aim at 'reviving some traits of these ideas using the memories of the spectators, and to ensure that one believes oneself to be transported back in time to an era and climate far away from us'. From 1775 onwards, Marie Antoinette had the gardens of the Petit Trianon landscaped and dotted with farm buildings.

René Louis de Girardin, Marquis of Vauvray, moved to his Ermenonville estate in 1766 after having travelled to Italy, Germany and England, where he was profoundly impressed by the Leasowes family estate, a park designed by William Shenstone, a poet and one of the earliest practitioners of landscape gardening. After having begun designing the landscape of Ermenonville (in Oise) with architect Jean-Marie Morel, whose preference was an idealisation of the natural landscape and rural architecture, Girardin started evolving his own ideas, introducing mills, designed to affirm and recall new moral values at the heart of his pictorial compositions. Very sympathetic to the ideas developed by Jean-Jacques Rousseau in his *On the Social Contract; or, Principles of Political Rights* published in 1762, Girardin welcomed the philosopher to his estate.[9] A few months later, when Rousseau died on 2 July 1778, the Marquis buried his embalmed body on the Île des Peupliers, part of the Ermenonville

Mausoleum at Castle Howard, North Yorkshire, 1699–1712 (architect: John Vanbrugh)

Needle's Eye, Wentworth, South Yorkshire, late 18th century (architect: John Carr)

Funeral inscription for Ringwood, an otter dog (early 19th century) on an 18th-century grotto at Rousham House

estate. The following year, the remains of the philosopher were placed in an antique-style tomb designed by Hubert Robert.

Also in 1779, the Alsatian artist and poet Georges-Frédéric Meyer, who painted pastoral scenes and the famous portrait of Jean-Jacques Rousseau gathering flowers, died at Ermenonville, having spent the last years of his life on the estate. He was buried under a headstone bearing the inscription 'Here lies George-Friederich Mayer, born in Strasbourg, he was a skilled painter and an honest man.'[10]

In France, the number of landscaped gardens incorporating references to the dead (whether a celebrity or a loved one) proliferated, and the Île des Peupliers became a site of pilgrimage. The composition inspired the Prince of Anhalt-Dessau, who had an identical reproduction made at Wörlitz (the present-day Garden Kingdom of Dessau-Wörlitz), the largest landscaped garden in continental Europe, which was planned by the architect Friedrich Wilhelm von Erdmannsdorff from 1790 onwards.

Pyramid at Branitz Park and Palace, Cottbus, 1856–7 (created by Count Hermann von Pückler-Muskau)

Tumulus pyramid at Branitz Park and Palace, Cottbus, 1860–63 (created by Count Hermann von Pückler-Muskau)

Garden Kingdom of Dessau-Wörlitz, Saxony-Anhalt (garden design: Prince Leopold III Friedrich Franz von Anhalt-Dessau)

Alexandre de Laborde, author of the *Description des nouveaux jardins de la France et de ses anciens châteaux*, published in 1808, cast a humorous and objective eye on the gardens of the previous generation.[11] He sniggered at the 'the heteroclite arrangement of the multiplication of temples, pagodas and ruins' and unavoidable references to death. 'Garden-makers absolutely required a deceased [...], and when one was not lucky enough to have one, one borrowed one from history.'[12] Alongside what he finds excessive, his book illustrates some extraordinary ways of evoking death in landscaped gardens. He gives examples from country houses in the Oise, including the tomb in the gardens of the Château du Plessis-Chamant, the '*vallée des tombeaux*' of the Château de Mortefontaine and, as is apt here, the Tomb of the Unknown and the Philosopher's Pyramid at Ermenonville.

During the eighteenth century, elements of death were also associated with the gardens of artists and writers. In his garden on the banks of the river Ilm in Weimar, Johann Wolfgang von Goethe created a landscape as a tribute to Christine von Lassberg, an abandoned lover who in 1778 drowned herself with a copy of *The Sorrows of Young Werther* in her pocket. As travellers brought new ideas back from England and books about English gardens started circulating in Europe, many landscape creations and treaties started being published in German and other languages. Following his *Remarques pour les maisons de campagne & l'art des jardins* published in Germany in 1773, Christian Cay Lorenz Hirschfeld produced the *Théorie de l'art des jardins*, a three-volume, bilingual French–German theoretical approach and description of various European gardens, which appeared between 1779 and 1785.[13] A chapter of twenty or so pages is dedicated to monuments, mausoleums and inscriptions, so many 'very efficient means of transmitting the memory of a person or an event to the following generations'. An astonishingly modern observation notes that 'a mausoleum does not seem to allow many ornaments'. The dissemination of the English model in Germany (and throughout Europe) raised questions of identity, provoking some to wonder what a German garden would look like.[14] Johann Jakob Atzel dreamed what this might be in his *Idéal d'un jardin allemand*.[15] Published in 1783, his book consists of a succession of images (which to us today might resemble a comic book or a cinematic tracking shot) depicting the heart of a thick forest peopled with broken idols and showing an abundance of tombs and ruins, which evoke the crucial moments in the construction of a German mythology: Charlemagne's tomb built on the debris of the destroyed Irminsul; a Gothic mausoleum; the cave of Holy Roman Emperor Frederick I, not dead, but asleep; the graves of other heroes; the urns of a chivalric poet and of numerous kings and emperors. Finally, Atzel describes: 'on a raised square, we see a huge tomb where the graves of Luther and Melanchthon lie side by side. Around this hill, various scenes recalling Heaven show works erected to the memory of worthy Germans of more recent times.' The will to affirm a specific type for 'the German Garden' remained crucial for Johann Christian August Grohman in his *Nouvelle théorie du bel art des jardins* (1797). But times were changing. If 'art could not manifest itself differently for princes and the bourgeois', it was precisely because the author was addressing the latter. The size of estates had changed: 'German gardens are small', 'they are not large or vast [...], and therefore require less means. The garden is no longer planted with conifers adapted to wide expanses, but includes foreign and exotic species of the plant kingdom', which fascinated garden lovers across Europe.

Regarding the dead resulting from war, we should note an initiative that was remarkable for the time, even though it was not followed through. Given the huge influx of military victims of the first two Silesian Wars (1740–42 and 1744–5), King Frederick the Great ordered the construction of an invalids' hospice for the wounded Prussian officers, the '*lahme Kriegsleut*' ('mutilated soldiers'), in Berlin. The buildings, erected on a 134-hectare estate known to Berliners as the 'Sahara', were completed in 1746 and the surroundings gardens were maintained by the convalescing soldiers. In 1748, a cemetery, the Invalidenfriedhof, was created for the burial of officers of the Prussian Army.[16] We can note some evolution in the burial methods for soldiers who died in combat during the eighteenth century. The great royal armies were starting to make provisions in their regulations, most often drawing their inspiration from the practices of antiquity. **M.R.**

---

1 Letter to George Selwyn, 12 August 1772, in *The Letters of Horace Walpole, Earl of Orford* (Philadelphia: Lea & Blanchard), 1844, vol. 2, p. 397.

2 John Dixon Hunt and Peter Willis (eds), *The Genius of the Place: The English Landscape Garden 1620–1820* (Cambridge, MA: The MIT Press), 1988.

3 See Patrizia Granziera, 'Freemasonic Symbolism and Georgian Gardens', *Esoterica: The Journal of Esoteric Studies* 5 (2003), pp. 42–72.

4 Vitruvius's *De architectura* (probably written between 30 and 15 BCE; first published in 1486) was first translated into English in the late seventeenth century.

5 John Dixon Hunt, *'Ut pictura poesis, the picturesque, and John Ruskin'*, MLN 93/5 (December 1978), pp. 794–818.

6 As in the previously mentioned Temple of British Worthies.

7 The number of memorials dedicated to animals – and more specifically war animals (the number of animals that died during the First World War is estimated to have been 9 million) – continues to grow to this day. The Animals in War Memorial, on London's Park Lane, was erected as a homage to all the animals that died while serving the British forces throughout history and was inaugurated in 2004. In 2018 the members of the Zoopolis association were granted the authorisation to build, in Paris, a monument to the animals that died during both world wars. There is also a memorial dedicated to the animals that died during the First World War, inaugurated in 2017 by representatives of the Australian War Animal Memorial Organization in Pozières, a small village in the Somme.

8 For the early developments, see Jean Ehrard, 'Nature et jardins dans la pensée française du 18e siècle', *Dix-huitième siècle* 1/45 (2013), pp. 365–77.

9 Jean-Jacques Rousseau, *Du contrat social; ou, Principes du droit politique*, Amsterdam, 1762.

10 *'Hier liegt George-Friederich Mayer, aus Straßburg geburtig, er war ein geschickter Mahler und ein redlicher Mann.'*

11 Alexandre de Laborde, *Description des nouveaux jardins de la France et de ses anciens châteaux* (Paris: Delance), 1808. De Laborde was son of the Marquis Jean-Joseph de Laborde, who had gardens created at his Château de Méréville, where Hubert Robert designed a cenotaph as a tribute to the English explorer James Cook. Alexandre de Laborde described the cenotaph, 'surrounded by many "foreign" trees that seem to reproduce the wild and faraway countries, which hide the true grave of the illustrious traveller' (ibid.).

12 Ibid.

13 C. C. L. Hirschfeld, *Théorie de l'art des jardins* (Leipzig: Héritiers de M. G. Weidmann et Reich), 1781; Minkoff Reprint, Geneva, 1973.

14 Stéphanie de Courtois, Marie-Ange Maillet and Eryck de Rubercy (eds), *Esthétique du jardin paysager allemand, XVIIIe–XIXe siècle* (Paris: Klincksieck), 2018.

15 Johann Jakob Artzel, *Ideal of a German garden: Une esquisse* (1783), quoted in ibid.

16 The first to be buried was a Catholic non-commissioned officer.

# FROM GARDEN TO MEMORIAL GARDEN

## From the 'revolution of cemeteries' to memorial gardens[1]

*Every citizen has the right to be buried regardless of race or religion.*
NAPOLEON BONAPARTE,
FIRST CONSUL OF THE FRENCH REPUBLIC

A series of reforms in France over a period of 25 years that resulted from the development of attitudes about the afterlife, the increase of city deaths, the spectre of pollution and odours,[2] the wish to put an end to burials within churches and adjoining cemeteries and to keep the image of death far away from towns, defined the framework in which a radically new landscape for the cemetery was to be invented. These graveyards would make evident the strong influence of the picturesque garden and the memorialisation of the deceased. Whereas, in the 1770s, cemeteries were unhealthy bare fields and places where individual identity disappeared, within just a few decades they became open spaces planted with trees, places of memory that were ideal for strolling in.

Following on from the Royal Decree of 10 March 1776, which limited *ad sanctos* burials and was to lead to the creation of *extra muros* cemeteries, Napoleon's Imperial Decree on Burials of 12 June 1804 took the graveyard away from the Church's space and authority. Burial grounds were now controlled by the municipal mayor. Simultaneously a 'novelty of the revolutionary era'[3] – inspired by the 1789 Declaration of the Rights of the Man and of the Citizen (such as 'Men are born free and remain free and equal in rights') – and the 'founding deed of a new cult of the dead',[4] Napoleon's decree restored everyone's right to a gravestone erected in the memory of the deceased. Decent burials were now the right of most social classes. At the same time, the landscaping of the new cemeteries was based on the cult of the dead that remained thriving in picturesque gardens, while shifting the sacred towards nature and in the process transforming it into an edifying art form.

In spring 1800, Lucien Bonaparte, Minister of the Interior and brother of Napoleon, requested that the Institut de France, the republic's scholarly association, organise a national competition for funerals and burials as 'the graves in cities present a hideous spectacle'. Forty proposals responded to the call: 'What ceremonies should be carried out for funerals and what rules should be enforced for places of burial?' Except for some monumental funerary projects designed by Claude-Nicolas Ledoux and by Étienne-Louis Boullée during the pre-Revolutionary era,[5] and leaving aside Pierre Martin Giraud's huge collective tomb made up of a central pyramid surrounded by a portico and a crematory oven for the vitrification of the bones of the dead, most of the proposals were very different from anything seen before. The first prize was shared by Amaury Duval and Abbé François-Valentin Mulot, who both preferred burials but did not exclude the pyre. Both laureates recommended that funerals be accompanied by music and flowering branches, and that cemeteries should be large planted areas without monuments. There should be no large stone tombs, just modest inscriptions by the graves, and prairies, streams and trees. In other words, the cemetery should be like the English landscaped garden treasured by philosophers and poets in the second half of the previous century.[6]

Although the old garden surrounding the house of François d'Aix de La Chaize (known as Père Lachaise)[7] was half abandoned, it was wooded and thus deemed perfectly suited to the creation of a new cemetery in 1804 by Alexandre-Théodore Brongniart,

Étienne-Louis Boullée, *Projet d'entrée d'un cimetière*, drawing, 1780, Paris, Bibliothèque nationale de France

architect and a general inspector of public works.[8] According to Brongniart, 'this place was suited to every state, every human opinion, [...] it could inspire religious sentiments devoid of terror to some, and to all would inspire respect, contemplation without sadness and, lastly, a form of melancholic charm resulting from the surrounding nature and placement of its monuments'.[9] He decided to include a Jewish cemetery and individual plots and to incorporate a pre-existing communal grave. He noted on his plan that he was 'forced to comply with existing planting'. Designed in keeping with the Anglo-Chinese gardens fashionable in the late eighteenth century, the general plan comprises a structure of regular alleys with one curving path in the middle, from which a network of small serpentine alleys unfold.[10] From the monumental portal, the whole is ordered around an esplanade bordered with a double row of trees and two alleys leading to the centre of the composition: the funeral chapel shaped like a huge red ochre pyramid. With its decoration of winged hourglasses in medallions and garlands of flowers absolutely devoid of religious associations, the main entrance designed by architect Étienne-Hippolyte Godde is part of the imagery of a cemetery that is open to all beliefs.[11]

In 1817 it was decided to bury national figures such as Molière, La Fontaine, Héloïse and Abélard in the Cemetery of the East (later known as Père Lachaise), in order to promote it. This decision would prove hugely successful. The idea of 'erecting the busts of the great men in the gardens, among the flowers and the trees' responded to a suggestion by the poet Jacques Delille and offered a new way of delaying the loss of the collective memory about death, while also giving the living the opportunity for a romantic stroll in a landscaped garden. At the same time it was a way of encouraging prestigious neighbours to buy plots. Adapted to new collective attitudes that had come about through changes in society, this new landscaping concept allowed the bourgeois of all religious denominations to acquire a piece of eternity for the price of a concession. This rapidly made Père Lachaise an international reference point throughout the nineteenth century for designers of new cemeteries in continental Europe, Britain and the United States.

In order to help fund the burying of the poor – a responsibility of the Church before the Revolution – Nicolas Frochot, Prefect of the Seine Department, introduced a tax levied on the funeral processions of the upper classes. In 1887 the 'Law on the freedom of funerals' was finally voted in and the first crematorium was built at the Père Lachaise Cemetery. Moreover, the population growth of the capital made necessary the creation of new cemeteries outside its city limits: the Passy Cemetery was established in the west in 1820, the Montparnasse Cemetery in the south in 1824, and the Montmartre Cemetery in the north in 1825. **M.R.**

Étienne-Louis Boullée, *Tombeau des Spartiates*, drawing, 1780, Paris, Bibliothèque nationale de France

Alexandre-Théodore Brongniart, *Projet pour le cimetière du Père-Lachaise*, undated, watercolour and black ink on paper, Musée Carnavalet, Paris

Entrance of Père Lachaise Cemetery, Paris, 1825 (architect: Étienne-Hippolyte Godde)

1 'Revolution of cemeteries' is a term used by Michel Vovelle and Régis Bertrand in *La Ville des morts: Essai sur l'imaginaire urbain contemporain d'après les cimetières provençaux* (Paris: Éditions du CNRS), 1983.

2 Alain Corbin, *Le miasme et la jonquille: L'odorat et l'imaginaire social, XVIIIe–XIXe siècles* (Paris: Flammarion), 1982.

3 *Guide du cimetière du Père-Lachaise* of 1836, quoted in Philippe Ariès, *L'homme devant la mort* (Paris: Éditions du Seuil), 1977.

4 Ariès, op. cit.

5 Étienne-Louis Boullée presented his celebrated Cenotaph to Turenne project in 1782.

6 Michel Ragon, *L'espace de la mort: Essai sur l'architecture, la décoration et l'urbanisme funéraires* (Paris: Albin Michel), 1981.

7 François d'Aix de La Chaize (1624–1709), a Jesuit priest, was the confessor of Louis XIV from 1675 until shortly before his death.

8 Alexandre-Théodore Brongniart (1739–1813) was a student of Étienne-Louis Boullée. He is buried at Père Lachaise Cemetery, which he himself had designed.

9 *Plans du palais de la Bourse de Paris et du cimetière Mont-Louis, en six planches, par Alexandre-Théodore Brongniart, architecte; Précédés d'une Notice sur ces Plans et sur quelques autres travaux du même Artiste* (Paris : Imprimerie Crapelet), 1814.

10 For Anglo-Chinese gardens, see Georges-Louis Lerouge, *Les jardins anglo-chinois, 1775–1788* (Paris: Connaissance et Mémoire), 2004 (first published 1779).

11 See Pascale Trompette and Robert Howell Griffiths, 'L'économie morale de la mort au XIXe siècle: Regards croisés sur la France et l'Angleterre', *Le Mouvement social* 4/237 (2011), pp. 33–54.

# GARDENS OF AN ALTERNATIVE ETERNITY

## Between Gothic and Egyptian Revival: England's denominational and nondenominational garden cemeteries

In the early nineteenth century the development of new types of cemeteries in Europe and the United States was characterised by the desire to respond to urgent factors concerning hygiene, which had been driven by Enlightenment ideas and the introduction of a commercial aspect in managing burials. It was a question of responding to the hope for equal treatment – often a source of conflict – between the dominant religions and the others, such as freethinkers in Belgium and Nonconformists (or Dissenters) in England and the United States. In England, from the early seventeenth century onwards, all Protestants who did not conform to the Anglican Church governance were entitled to be buried in a nondenominational cemetery that was open to everyone, regardless of Christian conviction. Established in London in 1665, Bunhill Fields was the burial place of several artistic and political personalities, including William Blake (died 1827) and Daniel Defoe (died 1731).[1] The proposed closing of the burial ground due to overcrowding drove some Nonconformists, led by George Collison, to elaborate an alternative project, the celebrated Abney Park Cemetery, which was open to everyone who could afford a concession, since it came to be run on a strictly commercial basis.[2]

Opened in 1840, the site was planted by George Loddiges (1786–1846) in the form of an arboretum boasting many exotic species. The beliefs of Abney Park Cemetery's advocates are blatantly obvious as soon as one goes through the entrance designed in Egyptian Revival style and walks around the picturesque landscape punctuated with neoclassical monuments. The Rosary Cemetery, in Norwich, is a clear manifesto of the backers of a cemetery open to all, a group that exasperated the defenders of the Anglican and Victorian social order such as Augustus Pugin, a staunch supporter of the Gothic Revival style.[3] Created in 1839, Highgate Cemetery reconciled both trends, albeit somewhat unequally: on one side pathways are punctuated by Gothic tombs and, on the other, is an intriguing Egyptian Avenue.[4]

During the first half of the nineteenth century the architectural model of Paris's Père Lachaise Cemetery continued to carry weight in England. It influenced the project for London's General Cemetery of All Souls in Kensal Green, designed in 1824 by Richard Forrest for the General Cemetery Company and inaugurated in 1832. That same year, the Metropolitan Cemetery Act introduced a commercial dimension to the construction and management of burial places. Glasgow Necropolis (1832) and Highgate Cemetery (1839) fell within the same landscaping and commercial scope. In 1843, the social reformer Edwin Chadwick compiled an 'Inventory of 174 churchyards' in the City of London.[5] This gives some idea of the wide range of beliefs and religious practices in existence at the time: included in the inventory are 13 burial plots dedicated to Congregationalists, 7 to Baptists, 5 to Methodists, 3 to Roman Catholics, 3 to Quakers, 4 to Jews, 1 for a 'foreigner' (a Swedish chapel it would seem), 16 for those 'without affiliation' and 6 designated as 'General Burial-Grounds'.[6]

**M.R.**

---

1 'Bunhill Fields' comes from 'Bone Hill', referring to a remains repository from St Paul's Cathedral, which was created when the building underwent work in 1549.

2 The first nondenominational burial ground in England was the Rosary Cemetery in Norwich, established by the Nonconformist minister Thomas Drummond in 1819.

Thomas Christopher Hofland, *Sheffield's General Cemetery*, soon after its opening in 1836, etching *c.*1830, The British Museum, London

3 Augustus Welby Northmore Pugin (1812–1852), famous for designing the interior and Big Ben of the Palace of Westminster, championed England's Gothic Revival style, which he deemed the only true Christian style. He embodied the opposition to the Gothic and Egyptian Revival style cemetery that was open to all and was the author of *An Apology for The Revival of Christian Architecture in England* (1843).

4 Church of England plots occupied 15 acres and Nonconformist plots occupied 2 acres.

5 *Cemetery Records: London Metropolitan Archives Information Leaflet Number 5*, City of London, 2015 <https://www.cityoflondon.gov.uk>.

6 Edwin Chadwick, *Report on the Sanitary Conditions of the Labouring Population of Great Britain. A Supplementary Report on the Results of a Special Inquiry into the Practice of Interment in Towns. [...]*, Printed by W. Clowes and Sons for Her Majesty's Stationery Office, London, 1843.

## From rural cemetery to urban park

During the eighteenth century, countless Europeans fled state religion and sailed to the United States. It is thus hardly surprising that the movement for cemeteries open to all should grow there, even earlier than it did in England. Following a competition held by the Massachusetts Horticultural Society, Mount Auburn Cemetery (near Boston) was initiated and conceived in 1815 by doctor and botanist Jacob Bigelow (1787–1879). Once purchased, the 70-hectare site outside the city limits became a cemetery laid out according to a landscaped garden

Mount Auburn Cemetery, Boston: Egyptian Revival portal (top) and neo-Gothic-style chapel (bottom), inaugurated in 1831

plan, criss-crossed with paths meandering between large bushes, lakes and groves.[1] Dedicated in 1831, the cemetery welcomed all faiths, while its commercial purpose and romantic landscape enabled the living to express themselves freely in marble and granite to celebrate the memory of the deceased. They did so in an innovative funeral art that embraced both an affirmation of beliefs and new emotions evoked by secular poetic expression.

Bigelow designed the monumental Egyptian Revival style entrance, which echoed the multifaith character of the new burial ground. Yet, mindful of religious sensitivities, he designed the funeral chapel inside the cemetery in the Gothic Revival dear to the religious authorities. Simultaneously responding to the expectations of the city's inhabitants and the preoccupations of those pushing for public health reform, the concept proved considerably successful and befitting the development of nineteenth-century American metropolises. The first guidebook of the Mount Auburn Cemetery, published in 1839, includes a description of some of its remarkable monuments and a collection of poems on death written by Nathaniel Hawthorne and Willis Gaylord Clark.[2] Following Mount Auburn, during the period up to 1860, multireligious cemeteries adopted the Egyptian Revival style for portals, tombs and other monuments, reflecting the era's fondness for this particular architectural movement.[3] In the previous century, impacted by images gleaned during Napoleon's Egyptian Campaign (1798–1801) and wanting to differentiate themselves in terms of beliefs, Freemasons in Europe filled their gardens with references to Egypt, which encouraged the adoption of the Egyptian Revival style in architecture and landscape.

Bigelow's choice of architectural style was to influence the form of the portal at London's Abney Park Cemetery (1840) and various other sites in the United States, including New Haven's Grove Street Cemetery, the entrance of which was designed by the architect Henry Austin in 1845.[4] In the 1840s, along with Mount Vernon and the Niagara Falls, Mount Auburn became one of the nation's most popular tourist spots. In addition, the cemetery was adopted as a prototype for the many cemeteries built in many large cities under the term 'rural cemeteries' or 'garden cemeteries'.[5] Adopted in 1847, the Rural Cemetery Act permitted commercial burial grounds within the rural state of New York. These new burial places were enormous.[6] Compared with the 45 hectares of the Père Lachaise Cemetery, their scale makes them genuine green spaces at the doors of the city. As French landscape designer Édouard André noted of Cincinnati's vast Spring Grove Cemetery in 1879: 'Once we have ceased performing burials, after a few years the city of Cincinnati will own a magnificent park that will not have cost its inhabitants a single dollar.'[7] The 'rural cemeteries' movement thus participated in the trend of creating major public parks that spread across the United States. In 1863, once his proposal for New York's Central Park had been accepted (1857), and after the adoption of the California Rural Cemetery Act of 1859, the great landscape architect Frederick Law Olmsted was entrusted with the design of Oakland's Mountain View Cemetery, with views looking out across San Francisco Bay. He enjoyed complete creative freedom and confided to Irish garden designer William Robinson: 'I do not think that I could lay out a burial place without making conditions about monuments such as I fear few but Quakers would be willing to accept.'[8] **M.R.**

---

1 The plan was designed by Henry Alexander Scammell Dearborn (1783–1851), assisted by Alexander Wadsworth (1806–1898).

2 *The Picturesque Pocket Companion and Visitor's Guide through Mount Auburn* (Boston: Otis, Broaders and Company), 1839.

3 For example, the Washington Monument obelisk (initiated 1848), monuments and memorials in the Calvary Cemetery in Queens, NY (1848), and the Graceland Cemetery in Chicago (1860).

4 Inaugurated in 1797, Grove Street Cemetery was the United States' first private burial ground. It was arranged in family plots and divided up into three sections corresponding to the three churches of New Haven Green, with other areas reserved for strangers who might die in New Haven, for the destitute, for people of colour and for Yale College.

5 As Michel Vovelle has noted (Michel Vovelle and Régis Bertrand, *La Ville des morts: Essai sur l'imaginaire urbain contemporain d'après les cimetières provençaux* [Paris: Éditions du CNRS], 1983), there is nothing rural about the 'rural cemetery'. The term draws its origins from the parks around big cities that created a transition between the urban and the genuine rural landscape. The persistence of the term may be partly due to the attachment of new citizens to the traditional 'churchyard' (or 'parish enclosure') and its rural origins.

6 Some examples: Laurel Hill, Philadelphia, 80 ha in 1835 (John Norman); Greenwood Cemetery, Brooklyn, 167 ha in 1838 (David Douglass); Allegheny Cemetery, Pittsburgh, 108 ha in 1845; Spring Grove Cemetery, Cincinnati, 240 ha, including its remarkable arboretum, in 1844 (Howard Daniels), transformed into a naturalistic park by Adolphe Strauch in 1855; Mountain View Cemetery, Oakland, 91 ha in 1863 (Frederick Law Olmsted); Bellefontaine Cemetery, near St. Louis, 141 ha in 1865; Lake View Cemetery, Cleveland, 121 ha in 1870.

7 Édouard André, *L'art des jardins: Traité général de la composition des parcs et jardins* (Paris: G. Masson), 1879, p. 790.

8 Quoted in Charles E. Beveridge and Paul Rocheleau, *Frederick Law Olmsted: Designing the American Landscape* (New York: Universe Publishing/Rizzoli), 1998.

Entrance of the New Haven Cemetery, 1839–48, engraving and watercolour on paper, Henry Austin Papers, Manuscripts and Archives, Yale University Library

Entrance portal, Abney Park Cemetery, East London, 1840 (architect: William Hosking)

The Egyptian Avenue, Highgate Cemetery, North London, 1839 (architect: Stephen Gear)

## Loudon's modern cemetery

In the early eighteenth century, Scottish garden designer John Claudius Loudon (1783–1843) was dismayed to find that some landscaped cemeteries remained devoid of drainage and had no method for preventing noxious vapours. A prolific author who instigated horticultural journals and championed the term 'landscape gardening', Loudon was also the inventor of the 'gardenesque', a style where attention was given to the individual plant and its placement according to the best conditions for growth, and the planting of exotic plants inside very simple geometric shapes.[1] In connection with his work as an urban planner, he suggested installing green spaces within London to improve the city's air quality and the use of solar energy for workers' dwellings.[2] Before designing cemeteries, Loudon was one of the first to affirm his principles on funerary monuments with great freedom of thought. After the death of his parents, he ordered the construction of a pyramid-shaped memorial in the spirit of Egypt, a style that was then favoured by freethinkers.[3] Loudon particularly liked Abney Park Cemetery with its Egyptian Revival portal. In his book on planting and cemetery management written shortly before his death, Loudon explained the origin of his interest in cemeteries.[4] Having seen for himself the appalling burial conditions of soldiers and citizens who had died during the Napoleonic Wars, he wrote: 'Our own attention was first forcibly directed to the subject of cemeteries in the year 1813; when [...] we visited the public cemetery at Warsaw [just after the Battle of Bautzen],[5] and saw there the coffins of the higher classes inserted in cells in the boundary wall, and hermetically sealed with stucco [...], while the poor were buried in trenches in the open ground, without coffins. [...] a little farther in the country, we saw the bodies of the aged poor, whose relatives could not afford either a coffin or the churchyard fees, dropped from the parish coffin into holes dug by the road side. The strong impression made by these scenes has induced us ever since to pay particular attention to cemeteries and churchyard wherever we have been, either abroad or at home [...].'[6]

While writing his manifesto for modern cemeteries, Loudon designed three radically new burial grounds.[7] In 1842 he designed the Histon Road Cemetery in Cambridge, one of the first cemeteries open to all faiths and a renewed model. The following year, Loudon devoted his last book to describing this type of cemetery, which was more rational and more economic in terms of land management and was founded on principles of efficient ventilation, since 'nothing is so desirable as to have a free current of air, and admit the drying influence of the sun'.[8] 'By scattering the trees and shrubs singly, graves may be everywhere formed among them; and, by placing trees continuously along the roads and walks, shade is afforded to those who are on them [...].'[9] Loudon recommends evergreens: 'The kind of trees we object to, because they are chiefly deciduous, and such as produce light-foliaged bulky heads, while fastigiate conical dark needle-leaved evergreens shade much less ground, produce much less litter when the leaves drop, and, by associations both ancient and modern, are peculiarly adapted for cemeteries.'[10] Clearly assigned into separate plots by orthogonal paths, the graves are easily accessible for visits and maintenance, which is made easier by planting conifers rather than deciduous trees. Chapels and other monuments should be placed at the main intersections and serve as landmarks. Loudon's very modern drawings prefigure the rigorous plans made by the Imperial War Graves Commission during the early twentieth century for future military cemeteries. Loudon's placement of chapels and other landmarks points to that of later memorials such as Reginald Blomfield's Cross of Sacrifice and Edwin Lutyens's Stone of Remembrance, which were installed repeatedly in the Commission's Commonwealth war cemeteries. However, in the 1870s the English horticultural community rejected the Loudonesque sombre alliance of conifers and rectilinear paths, and championed informal tracery and flower-filled meadows, a bucolic tendency echoed by some German park cemeteries.[11] **M.R.**

---

1 Loudon's journals included *The Encyclopaedia of Gardening* (1822), *The Encyclopaedia of Agriculture* (1825), *The Gardener's Magazine* (the first periodical dedicated to horticulture, founded in 1826) and *Magazine of Natural History* (1828).

2 John Claudius Loudon, 'Hints for Breathing Places for the Metropolis, and for Country Towns and Villages, on fixed Principles', *The Gardener's Magazine* 5 (1829), pp. 686–90.

3 The so-called Loudon memorial is in the churchyard of St John the Baptist, Pinner, Middlesex. Uncommonly, halfway up the pyramid is a fake sarcophagus, an incredibly free interpretation of the family wish that stipulated that Loudon's parents would leave a sum of money if their bodies were maintained above ground. In reality, their corpses are buried in a grave beneath the pyramid.

4 John Claudius Loudon, *On the Laying Out, Planting, and Managing of Cemeteries; and on the Improvement of Churchyards* (London: Longman, Brown, Green, and Longmans), 1843.

5 8,500 soldiers died during the Battle of Bautzen, which opposed Napoleonic troops and the Russian–Prussian army during 20–21 May 1813.

6 Loudon, op. cit., 'Preface', p. iii.

7 Histon Road Cemetery (Cambridge, UK), Bath Abbey Cemetery (on a hillside overlooking Bath) and Southampton Old Cemetery (the plan of which was eventually rejected, as the Bishop of Winchester did not want a Church of England chapel to be situated adjacent to a Nonconformist chapel).

8 Loudon, op. cit., p. 69.

9 Loudon, op. cit., p. 69.

10 Loudon, op. cit., p. 69.

11 Such as Cologne's Südfriedhof (South Cemetery), conceived by Johannes Ibach in 1899. See Brent Elliott, 'Cemetery', *The Oxford Companion to the Garden* (Oxford/New York: Oxford University Press), 1986, p. 101.

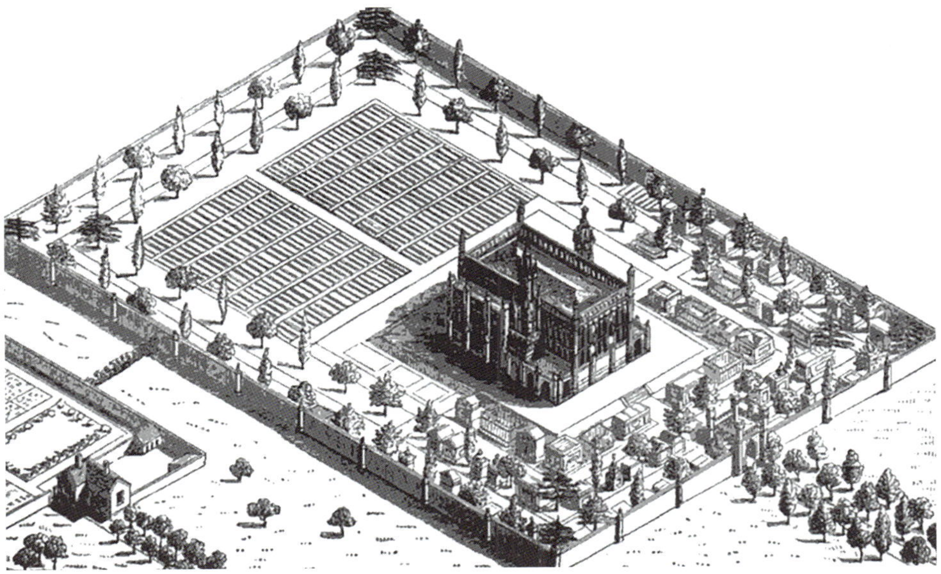

The tomb of John Claudius Loudon's parents, William (died 1809) and Agnes (died 1831), in Pinner churchyard, Middlesex

'Isometrical view of a churchyard adapted for an agricultural parish', from John Claudius Loudon, *On the Laying Out, Planting, and Managing of Cemeteries; and on the Improvement of Churchyards*, London, 1843

# THE INVENTION OF THE WAR CEMETERY AND THE MEMORIAL TO THE MISSING

## A pioneer initiative during the American Civil War

Having experienced the resurgence of the cult of the dead in the landscape gardens of Europe during the eighteenth century, the evolution of civilian cemeteries that followed the creation of the Père Lachaise Cemetery in Paris, and the growing popularity of garden cemeteries in America and England, when it came to the great wars of the nineteenth century and the first conflicts using so-called industrial warfare, the fate of the corpses of soldiers who had died in combat and the memory of their names could no longer be ignored. During the American Civil War (1861–5) the very high number of fallen soldiers, the repatriation of wounded men who would for the most part die of their injuries, and the deaths of very young men – often, due to conscription, members of the same family – all contributed to society calling into question everyone, but also public authorities.[1]

The development of the press was to ignite this collective doubt. The lack of appropriate spaces made the problem all the more urgent since neither rural cemeteries nor traditional churchyards had enough space to accommodate such high numbers of bodies. The issue could no longer remain unresolved. New ideas had made their way westwards, particularly those stemming from the French Revolution: 'Men are born and remain free and equal in rights' and 'Everyone is entitled to a headstone'.[2]

On 16 July 1862, in the midst of the American Civil War, under the presidency of Abraham Lincoln, Congress made a clean break with the principle of common graves. From then on, the soldiers of the Union Army were to be buried in individual graves whenever the bodies were able to be identified.[3] Moreover, the headstones were to bear the same marks, regardless of rank, social origin or religion. The following year, the government started purchasing plots of land and military cemeteries were created. Two years after Congress's decision, Arlington National Cemetery in Virginia received the first corpses of fallen soldiers. The first large cemeteries were located near to battlefields and hospitals. Chattanooga (Tennessee), which was established in 1863 on the order of Major General George Henry Thomas in the aftermath of the battles that ravaged the surrounding area, became a National Cemetery in 1867. By 1870 it already had 12,000 graves, including bodies from other conflicts, such as the 1,500 dead in the Battle of Chickamauga.

In 1867 a law compelled the War Secretary to ensure that each headstone was engraved with a name and that there was a superintendent on site to manage the cemetery. The model of the identifying stone was adopted in 1873. The same year, eligibility for burial in a National Cemetery was broadened to include all veterans. In the 1870s, a total of 300,000 Confederate soldiers and sailors were buried in 73 National Cemeteries. By the end of the American Civil War, 30 National Cemeteries had been created and seven plots for soldiers had been created in private graveyards.[4]

Today there are more than 175 National Cemeteries, soldiers' plots, government plots and Confederate cemeteries managed by three federal agencies: the National Cemetery Administration of the United States Department of Veterans Affairs, the United States Department of the Army within the United States Department of Defense, and the National Park Service. For people of American origin, interment in a National Cemetery is authorised for all members of the armed forces, their spouses, the widows or widowers of veterans, and minors.

While during conflict the urgency consists in improving the living conditions of active soldiers and taking care of the wounded through public health channels, the question of cemeteries raises its head in the aftermath of war. Landscape architect Frederick Law Olmsted was in charge of directing the US Sanitary Commission, a private humanitarian organisation created in 1861 to help the wounded and improve the sanitary conditions of volunteers in the Union Army troops. This was inspired by the British Sanitary Commission created during the Crimean War (1853–6) and the Red Cross, created in 1863.[5] After the Civil War, monuments to the dead were sometimes designed on the initiative of the municipalities. From 1879 to 1882, in North Easton, Massachusetts, Olmsted created The Rockery (also known as the Memorial Cairn), a memorial for the city's citizens lost in the American Civil War, which included soldiers and sailors. The idea was that children should tend the flowers on the cairn. **M.R.**

1 600,000 died during the four years of the American Civil War.

2 Declaration of the Rights of Man and of the Citizen, 1789, Article I; Imperial Decree on Burials, 12 June 1804, Article 12.

3 Soldiers did not bear any identification except for a scrap of paper with their name and address pinned to their clothes. Metal identity tags (dog tags) did not appear until the twentieth century.

4 The resting places for combatants who had fought in conflicts in which United States servicemen were engaged.

5 The Red Cross was co-founded by the humanitarian Henry Dunant who in 1859 had witnessed the aftermath of the Battle of Solferino.

## Persistence of oblivion and recovered remembrance: the European wars of the nineteenth century

In spite of the emergence of a new cult of the dead testified by the growth of landscaped cemeteries for civilians in the first half of the nineteenth century, the interment and the remembrance of those killed in battle did not evolve much during the century. However, the 1856 Treaty of Paris, which ended the Crimean War, foresaw the preservation of military graves for the very first time. In practice, the British and the French continued to bury their dead in mass graves, unit by unit, and nothing had changed compared to previous centuries.

However, during the 1870–71 Franco-Prussian War, the situation evolved – at least for officers, who were buried in individual graves. But ordinary soldiers from both sides were still buried in communal graves near the battlefields. Almost 37,000 individual graves were dug in the 'military sections' marked out in the communal cemeteries. The future of these places of burial was defined by Article 16 of the Treaty of Frankfurt, which ended the war in 1871. Henceforth, the belligerents had to take charge of regrouping the graves and their perpetual care. In 1878, the fear that the collective memory of the fallen of the 1870–71 war might fade, resulted in a decision by the Reich to create an identity plaque for each soldier. Similar measures were taken by France in 1881. This aimed to facilitate identification of soldiers on battlefields, easing the bereavement of families and the management of inherited estates. **M.R.**

## From the Boer War to the creation of the Imperial War Graves Commission

During the First World War and in the years that followed, the authorities of each belligerent country had to assume the responsibility of taking part in a conflict that had led millions of citizens to their deaths. They had to consider the demands of families and the population as a whole by administering burials and cemeteries. That the invention of war cemeteries and memorials sprung from the British Empire is no coincidence. Initiated in the early eighteenth century with the subject of death appearing in landscape gardens, debates thrived in the United States and in Britain around the design of graveyards that should be adapted to new ideas, particularly in relation to different faiths. In addition to the 1862 American Congress commitment to grant burials in individual graves, the experience of the British in South Africa during the Second Boer War (1899–1902) proved useful.[1] In the aftermath of the conflict, the Britain authorities were confronted with the demand that they should honour their citizens, who had volunteered to fight in this faraway war. The government showed its respect for its soldiers by allocating them individual graves in cemeteries and by creating memorials to the fallen soldiers that were designed as sacrificial grounds, like so many other sacred areas near battlefields.

Several members of a small group of experts, who had fought together in South Africa and remained in touch, met in 1917 as the Imperial War Graves Commission (IWGC). It is to them that we owe the invention of the war cemetery and the memorial to the fallen that we still know today. Having served as Director of Education in the Transvaal Colony from 1900 until 1905, Major General Sir Fabian Ware (1869–1949) was the co-founder of the IWGC and became the unrelenting intermediary between the battlefields of the First World War and the civilian, military and religious authorities in London.[2] During and after the Second Boer War he was part of the renowned Milner's Kindergarten, a nickname given to a group of young Oxford University graduates recruited to the South African Civil Service by Alfred Milner, Governor of the Cape Colony and High Commissioner for South Africa. Entrusted with advising Milner on how to reorganise the administration of the Transvaal after the conflict, the group's members remained very close after their South African experience. Disciples of philosopher John Ruskin, they shared the same dream of a fusion

Oakwood Cemetery, Richmond, VA. Individual graves of Confederate soldiers who had died during the American Civil War, 1865, stereoscopic photography, Prints and Photographs Division, Library of Congress, Washington, DC

Graves of the war of 1870, Coincy, Aisne

Mass grave for British soldiers who died during the Battle of Spion Kop (23–24 January 1900), Second Boer War, South Africa

of socialism and capitalism, and an aspiration to bind new links between the United Kingdom and the autonomous governments of its colonies in the form of a federal union that would replace the British Empire. In 1909 they founded *The Round Table: The Commonwealth Journal of International Affairs* to spread their ideas based on the respect of different cultures and religions.

Some found themselves in the IWGC team in an era when Milner, who was much appreciated for his civilian management during the state of war in South Africa, was part of David Lloyd George's War Cabinet.[3] In the days of Milner's Kindergarten, they gathered in The Stonehouse in Parktown, Johannesburg, the private residence of Herbert Baker, who became one of the key architects for the IWGC from its creation until September 1928, and had designed The Stonehouse as his own home. Baker's South African experience in the area of military monuments was recognised during the animated discussions of the IWGC members and contributed in establishing his authority.

On the occasion of a commission by Cecil Rhodes, Baker reflected on the form that should be given to the Honoured Dead Memorial, in remembrance of those who had died during the Siege of Kimberley in the northern part of the Cape.[4] For this resolutely neoclassical colonial project, which was inaugurated in 1904, Baker took his inspiration from the architecture of the so-called Tomb of Theron, the Greek tyrant of Agrigento. During a trip to the Mediterranean, he made a sketch of this monument commemorating the thousands who had died during the siege of the city.[5] Asserting the imperial project to appropriate South Africa, the text carved in the memorial's Stone of Remembrance was commissioned from Rudyard Kipling:

> This for a charge to our children in sign
> of the price we paid.
> The price that we paid for freedom that
> comes unsoiled to your hand.
> Read, revere and uncover, here are
> the victors laid.
> They that died for their city being sons
> of the land.

Another future member of the IWGC, Kipling was also asked to choose the words that should be inscribed on the individual headstones. **M.R.**

---

1 The number killed in the Second Boer War is estimated to have been 53,000.

2 Transvaal is a former province in northeastern South Africa, north of the Vaal River.

3 Alfred Milner (1854–1925) was a member of the War Cabinet from December 1916 to November 1918.

4 Cecil Rhodes served as Prime Minister of South Africa's Cape Colony from 1890 to 1896.

5 Led by the Romans in 261 BCE during the First Punic War, against Carthage and Syracuse.

Tomb of Theron, Agrigento, built to pay homage to the dead of the Battle of Agrigentum in 261 BCE, Sicily

Honoured Dead Memorial, Kimberley, South Africa, 1904

## Fabian Ware and the inventors of a new remembrance landscape

When war broke out in 1914, Fabian Ware was too old to fight. Supported by Lord Alfred Milner, he was put in command of a mobile unit provided by the British Red Cross. Confronted by the huge difficulty of locating the bodies of hundreds of thousands of British soldiers hastily buried on the battlefields of all the fronts, which were sometimes gathered in makeshift cemeteries but very often isolated, Ware recorded the graves of the improvised cemeteries, a task encouraged by General Nevil Macready, with whom he had been in South Africa. Recognised in 1915 by the Imperial War Office and carried out under the auspices of the British Army's Graves Registration Commission, the inventory shows the magnitude of the task of honouring the multitude of fallen and missing soldiers on foreign land in various kinds of cemeteries. Organised on an *ad hoc* basis, this project would take years to complete.

In May 1917, the Imperial War Graves Commission (IWGC) was established by Royal Charter, with the Prince of Wales serving as president and Ware as vice-chairman. Ware called upon the leading architects of the period, including Sir Edwin Lutyens, Sir Herbert Baker and Sir Reginald Blomfield to design cemeteries. He commissioned the poet and novelist Rudyard Kipling to choose the epitaphs to be engraved on headstones and asked Sir Frederic Kenyon, Director of the British Museum, to gather together the various approaches in a report. Published in November 2018, this report defined the design of war graves, stressing the importance of equality of treatment of the dead who came from all around the world, the absence of crosses on the graves, the banning of religious symbols except for discreet emblems not visible from afar, the exclusion of sculptures and the importance of planting.[1] Each grave was to host a body: there would be no empty plots – or 'dud graves', as Kipling, whose son was missing, called them.[2] 'The grave is much more than a memorial [...] it is a container that refers to a content hidden from sight.'[3] The remembrance of the missing were to be honoured elsewhere, by collective memorials on which families would find the names of their dead relatives carved. The first choice was to create several small war cemeteries close to the battlefields, as opposed to the huge cemeteries that were being created by the French and the Germans, and to privilege fine landscaping. Despite the opinion of such political figures as Winston Churchill, who opposed 'vast expanses filled with uniform stones reminiscent of the markers found alongside roads', Lutyens advocated the grouping of graves to allow for 'a more beautiful treatment'. The Kenyon Report presented a first suggestion for associating tombs without headstones and a monument on which names are engraved: 'the cemetery would have the appearance of a small park or garden, composed of turf or flower beds divided by paths, planted with shrubs or trees, and in no way recognisable as a cemetery, except by the presence of some central monument or monuments'.[4]

In the second option, which was to be adopted, 'the cemetery [...] will be marked by rows of headstones of uniform height and width [...]. The graves themselves might, in principle, be either separate mounds or a continuous flat surface. In practice I strongly recommend the latter, as being both easier to maintain [...] and better adapted for decoration by flowers. The rows of headstones in their ordered ranks carry on the military idea, giving the appearance as of a battalion on parade'.[5] It must be kept in mind that the report was written by the English for the English, and therefore deeply impregnated with a culture of landscape and garden. By rejecting the first alternative, the members of the Commission ruled out the kind of park cemeteries that had been established in London and other cities during the nineteenth century. Indeed, these cemeteries would have proven very costly and unmanageable. In fact, the adopted concept and ensuing realisations over the next following years were surprisingly close to the pioneering vision of John Claudius Loudon in their general plan and placement of graves. They admirably took on the general spirit of the English cottage garden of the kind designed by Gertrude Jekyll around the houses of Lutyens, not only in terms of planting and flowers but in all other details of garden architecture.

The creators paid special attention to the type of stone chosen for the headstones and memorials and its relationship with the local landscape, and favoured low planting. Trees such as African oak, Canadian maple and Australian acacia were selected to evoke some of the tree landscapes familiar in each of the countries of the soldiers.

The great merit of the IWGC was its success, through teamwork supported by political authorities at critical moments, to consider the diversity of afterlife beliefs of soldiers who had come from all over the world and to define standard elements that made every British war cemetery instantly recognisable: the headstones, the Stone of Remembrance, the Great Cross of Sacrifice, the low wall and the register. The ecumenical principle of a single headstone shape and style of carving adapted to each faith came from afar: from the development of civil liberties in England and France in the eighteenth century; the development of ideas about burial conditions and even Napoleon's decree that 'Every citizen has the right to be buried regardless of race or religion'; the spread of nondenominational cemeteries in England and the United States in the nineteenth century; and up to and including the ideas of Milner's Kindergarten about respecting the various cultures and creeds of the British Empire. The preference for Portland stone for all the headstones had its origins in the use of this particular stone in countless emblematic public buildings, including London's St Paul's Cathedral and Buckingham Palace. It offered every deceased and their family a piece of architecture that would forever speak of England, a little bit like a stone or talisman picked up in one's childhood landscape and always kept in one's pocket.

Regarding headstones, the Kenyon Report stressed that two essential elements made up the 'mark of [...] a British cemetery of the Great War' and that these would be integrated into all compositions: Lutyens's Stone of Remembrance and the Cross are sited eastwards, as 'we are a Christian Empire'.[6] Raised on a three-stepped platform, the Stone of Remembrance is both an altar and a monumental grave facing the enemy to the east, and is an unalterable abstract form marked with the biblical inscription 'their name liveth for evermore', chosen by Kipling.[7] However, 'the [...] size, pattern, and position (of the Cross) would be left to the artist who designs each cemetery'.[8] Reflecting the IWGC's aspiration for ecumenism, Baker's design for a traditional cross with a sword and a bronze sailing ship was not chosen. Of his interpretation, a Cross with very short arms close to the form of the Celtic Cross, Blomfield commented, 'When I designed this Cross, I wanted it to be as abstract and impersonal as possible, to liberate it from all associations through a particular style.' Yet, a large bronze sword was to be added to reaffirm the alliance of the 'sabre and the flail', in the words of Georges Clemenceau. This alliance of the Cross and warrior symbols can be found in all the cemeteries and war memorials of the countries who fought in the First World War.

Another invention of the IWGC was the Memorial to the Missing, where we find the names of all the soldiers whose bodies were never recovered. Architects were to create more than 20 such memorials between 1920 and 1938. Each creation testified to the personality of the main architect, seen in the relationship between landscape and architecture, even in the tiniest details such as the spaces left between grass and stone.

There were four main architects: Herbert Baker (1862–1946), Edwin Lutyens (1869–1944), Reginald Blomfield (1856–1942) and Charles Holden (1875–1960). They worked with the partial and sometimes complete contribution of assistant architects: William Bryce Binnie (1886–1963), Wilfred Clement von Berg (1894–1978), William Harrison Cowlishaw (1869–1957), George Hartley Goldsmith (1886–1967), Frank Higginson (1890–1958), Arthur James Scott Hutton (1891–1982), George Esslemont Gordon Leith (1885–1965), Noel Ackroyd Rew (1880?), John Reginald Truelove (1886–1942), Henry Philip Cart de Lafontaine (1884–1963). There were also many artists associated with these projects, such as MacDonald Gill who oversaw the engraving on the headstones, plus blacksmiths and graphic designers.[9]

The creative team was dominated by the architects, including those that specialised in garden design. Blomfield and

Stone of Remembrance and Cross, Hooge Crater Cemetery, Zillebeke, 1918 (architect: Edwin Lutyens, assisted by John Truelove)

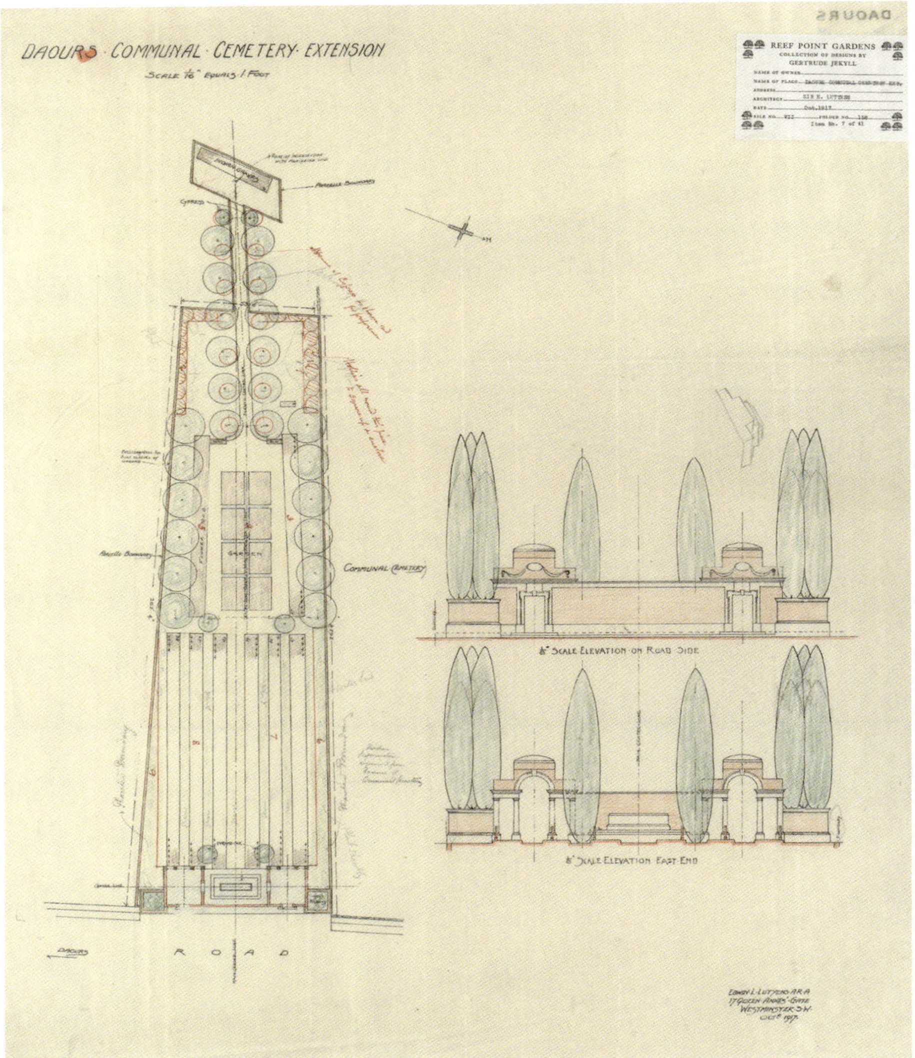



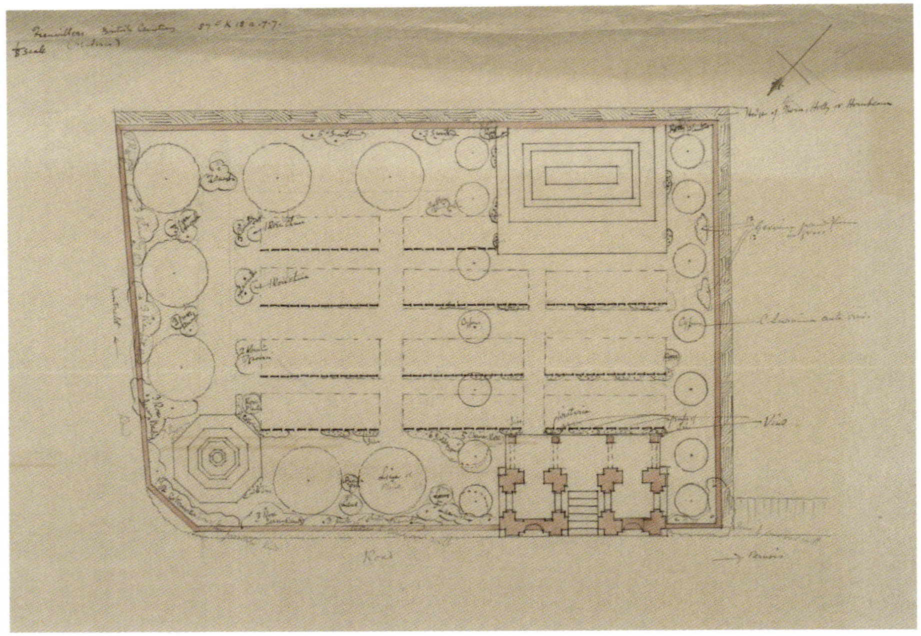

Gertrude Jekyll, *Daours Communal Cemetery Extension*, 1917, preliminary drawing, Gertrude Jekyll Collection, Environmental Design Archives, UC Berkeley

Gertrude Jekyll, *Fienvillers British Cemetery*, 1917, preliminary drawing, Gertrude Jekyll Collection, Environmental Design Archives, UC Berkeley

Lutyens were recruited for their very different approaches. Since the publication of his book *The Formal Garden in England* in 1892, and his myriad commissions for country houses with their assorted gardens, Blomfield had affirmed himself as a garden designer. He relentlessly opposed the informal planting and naturalistic gardens of William Robinson and promoted a garden designed in harmony with that of the house. 'We protest against the idea that there is an art of the house and an art of the garden. Both rest on the same principles and aim a common goal', he declared, even affirming that 'only architects have the intellectual capacity to design a garden – it is the task of gardeners to pick up gravel and grow gooseberries'. Besides these bold provocations, however, Blomfield also admitted that 'gardeners have said that architects knew nothing about gardening and that they knew nothing about design, and there was much truth on both sides'. As for Lutyens, he was already recognised for the many country houses that he had designed in collaboration with a famous gardener whose ideas echoed those of Robinson. Garden designer Gertrude Jekyll published a dozen reference books about gardens during the course of the IWGC's activities. The arrangement of plants was a crucial element underlined in the Kenyon Report: 'Much of the general effect of the cemeteries will depend on the planting, and it is essential that the architectural designers of the cemeteries should work in the closest cooperation with the horticultural experts.'[10]

As soon as it was created, the IWGC appointed Arthur Hill, botanist and assistant director of the Royal Botanic Gardens (Kew, London Borough of Richmond upon Thames), as its horticultural adviser. He was to remain so until his death in 1941, during which time he adapted planting for the First World War battlefields, not only in France and in Belgium, but also in Italy, Palestine, Greece, Turkey and Mesopotamia. Kenyon and Hill shared the idea that the 'restfulness of grass and the brightness of flowers in fitting combination would appear to strike the proper note of brightness and life'. In 1916, Hill visited the first British cemeteries in northern France, noting that in the absence of arable land some plants would not survive. He gave advice on the sowing of seeds and the planting of suitable trees and shrubs (such as *Cupressus lawsoniana intertexta*, *Berberis stenophylla*, *Mahonia aquifolium* and *Laburnum alpinum*).[11] Revisiting the sites of these cemeteries between 18 March and 8 April, Hill was delighted with the progress accomplished, considering that the 'annual seedlings were very precious in conveying some light to a desolate desert and encourage our men who wander or walk by a little bit of the English countryside and gardens'.

Hill himself drew a scheme comprising strips bordered with grass, where graves and lawns alternated. But in early 1918, confronted with the scale of the task, the botanist stressed that grass must not be planted if there were no means to maintain it. Also, having found that some volunteers were finding it difficult to work on their own without direction, he stated that it was necessary to organise their work more effectively. The following

year, Colonel Durham was assigned the job of directing informal work groups. He worked in close collaboration with Hill and, with a team of 362 gardeners working under him in 1921, became the essential link between the architect and the horticultural company. Mobile gardening groups created new cemetery gardens once the permanent constructions were completed, and nurseries were installed in France to grow the many plants required.

Although the spirit of Jekyll's gardens infused the British war cemeteries created after the war, there are no documents confirming her formal association with the IWGC. However, her significant influence on the IWGC gardeners can be detected, which came about through association, due to her many projects with Lutyens and her plethora of books and articles.[12] With her friend Lutyens, she worked as part of the IWGC teams and effectively participated in many of the projects, giving advice to Lutyens about planting, for instance. She had already designed the gardens surrounding more than three hundred of his houses and drew the planting plans for several of his cemeteries.[13] To lighten the mournfulness of the place and add a little affection from the young fallen's homeland, Jekyll suggested various plantings that would incorporate a piece of English garden at the foot of each headstone: 'a cut low edge, spring bulbs, a few rose bushes, clovers, *Skimmia*, *Buddleia*, *Clematis flammula*, *Aruncus*, Bergenita borders, white carnations and columbines associated with large patches of grass, sometimes a few shrubs in cluster or aligned'.

On each site these fields of headstones, each with their individual flowers, offer a peaceful presence while keeping alive the memory of the lives that ended there. Situated in a wide range of landscapes and climates, they testify to the contribution of English garden design to an exceptional remembrance project of the early twentieth century. For each of these British territories on French soil, the gardener is none other than the Imperial War Graves Commission (IWGC), which became the Commonwealth War Graves Commission (CGWC) in 1960. Everywhere around the globe, British cemeteries respond to rigorous criteria that allow for easy maintenance. Well after both world wars, their impeccable design is maintained at 23,000 memorial sites, in 150 countries, by more than 850 people, 459 of whom (including 320 gardeners in France alone) are in charge of maintaining 210 hectares of the gardens of peace, 65 kilometres of borders, several thousand rose bushes and hundreds of trees. After his visit to the Bois-Guillaume Communal Cemetery (on the outskirts of Rouen), on 14 March 1925, where he spoke with the head gardener, Rudyard Kipling wrote *The Gardener*, a short story that can be read as a tribute to all the gardeners of the IWGC, and their essential role in commemorating those resting under their protection.[14] After the war, families waited until the springtime to visit the cemetery, as they had done for their civilian dead, since 'the grave visited when covered in flowers takes on the function of a conduit for emotions, of support for the bereavement of families'.[15]

Today, visitors are still welcomed. They can enjoy the same kind of intimate peace as experienced in a private garden: they can see the cemetery from afar thanks to its low wall above which the Cross of Sacrifice emerges, access it through a wide entrance and a finely designed metal gate, consult the register of graves, shelter from the rain in a small pavilion or from the sun under a pergola covered with wisteria and climbing roses, reflect while sitting on a bench sited to offer the most soothing associations between this garden of peace and the changing colours of the country landscape with which it communes over the hours and seasons. **M.R.**

Terrace, Hestercombe Gardens, Somerset, 1904–6 (design: Edwin Lutyens and Gertrude Jekyll)

Mazargues British War Cemetery, Marseille, 1918 (architect: Arthur James Scott Hutton)

---

1 *War Graves. How the cemeteries abroad will be designed. Report to the Imperial War Graves Commission by Lieut.-Colonel Sir Frederic Kenyon, K.C.B., Director of the British Museum* (London: His Majesty's Stationery Office), 1918. The recommendations applied to graves for servicemen originating from countries around the world, including South Africa, Australia, New Zealand, Canada, China and India.

2 Kipling's son, John, was reported wounded and missing in action during the Battle of Loos in September 1915.

3 Régis Bertrand and Anne Carol (eds), *Aux origines des cimetières contemporains: Les réformes funéraires de l'Europe occidentale, XVIII$^{e}$–XIX$^{e}$ siècle* (Aix-en-Provence: Presses universitaires de Provence), 2016.

4 *War Graves. How the cemeteries abroad will be designed*, op. cit., pp. 13–14.

5 Ibid.

6 *War Graves. How the cemeteries abroad will be designed*, op. cit.

7 Book of Ecclesiasticus 44:14.

8 The form of the central Cross is not unlike that of the Hosanna Cross often found in French villages.

9 Frank Rambert provides the entire list: Frank Rambert, *Jardins de guerre: Les cimetières britanniques sur le front ouest* (Geneva: MetisPresses), 2014.

10 *War Graves. How the cemeteries abroad will be designed*, op. cit.

11 Sarah Joiner, 'The Evolution of the Planting Influences of the Imperial War Graves Commission from its Inception to the Modern Day', *Garden History* 42 (Autumn 2014), pp. 90–106.

12 Particularly the last book that she published before the war: Gertrude Jekyll and Lawrence Weaver, *Gardens for Small Country Houses* (London: Country Life), 1912.

13 In Somme: Auchonvillers Military Cemetery, La Neuville British Cemetery at Corbie, Daours Communal Cemetery Extension, Fienvillers British Cemetery, Gézaincourt Communal Cemetery Extension. In Pas-de-Calais: Hersin Communal Cemetery Extension, Warlincourt Halte British War Cemetery at Saulty.

14 Rudyard Kipling never found the body of his son, who died on 27 September 1915. *The Gardener* tells the story of a woman who finds the grave of her illegitimate son thanks to the help of the gardener, who understands that the body she seeks is not that of a nephew as she pretends, but that of her son.

15 Bertrand and Carol, op. cit.

## Ohlsdorf Cemetery, Hamburg (1877)

It is no coincidence that the first park cemeteries inspired by the English burial grounds were situated in cities of the former Hanseatic League, such as Kiel (1865–9), Bremen (1872–5) and Hamburg (1877).[1] Demographic pressure and new demands of public sanitation reformers urged elected officials to purchase, in 1874, a 90-hectare site in the village of Ohlsdorf, just outside Hamburg, mirroring the circumstances in other large cities. Trees and shrubs were planted to create enclosures and to enhance some sections designated for graves. Although 90 per cent of the plots were occupied by Lutherans, the cemetery was a nondenominational cemetery with access to all. The first burials took place in 1877, but the cemetery only took its final shape with the hiring of Wilhelm Cordes (1840–1917). His vision was applied to the detriment of the ideas of his predecessor and competitor, the engineer Franz Andreas Meyer, whose proposal for a general layout – inspired by London's Little Ilford Park (1856) – was deemed too costly. In 1881, Cordes was asked to submit an alternative plan that matched that of crematorium parks.

Cordes designed the space as a single 'landscape image' that encompassed several vistas in one whole. The project differed from those of its American counterparts since, in Cordes's view, the priority and practical aim must remain the grave, not the pleasure park. The water features are also drainage tanks, while mortuary chapels are multiplied to 'reduce the distance for the undertakers'. Likewise, a large central alley crosses the cemetery and serves the burial plots. This attention to functionality was considered virtuous, in accordance with the dominant demands of the bourgeoisie. A botanical garden, exotic species from the four corners of the globe, a 'historic' rose garden and a so-called 'geological' hill with alpine flowers completed the project. In 1897, Cortes wrote a guide to 'his' cemetery, which had reached an area of 186 hectares in 1900 when it was presented at the Paris World Fair, at the start of its international renown. However, success remained local and Ohlsdorf progressively became, against its creator's original wish, a place for excursions, a pleasure park where families came for a day out. In 1903 a social democrat newspaper noted that the cemetery 'reconciles visitors with death but also with life'. In 1917, after the death of Cordes, Otto Linne (1969–1937) oversaw the series of extensions that were to make Ohlsdorf the world's largest cemetery (404 hectares in 1933).

In addition to the historic dimension of its landscaping, the cemetery can be read as an open book of German memory. Around 3,400 German soldiers and other victims of the First World War are buried in a military section (1925) dominated by an imposing spruce, called the *Kriegertanne* (Warrior Fir). Identical headstones, reflecting the principle of equality in the face of death, vary in shape to avoid a heavy uniform style. In a relatively daring gesture for the time, Cordes had ordered rosebushes to be planted between the headstones. Having disappeared since then, they are now replaced by grass.

On two occasions – in 1915 and 1921 – architectural competitions were organised for the creation of war memorials. Walter Puritz (1882–1957) won both, although his final projects were ultimately rejected due to the required sobriety and disproportionate cost. In 1938, Robert Tischler (1885–1959), the chief architect of the Volksbund Deutsche Kriegsgräberfürsorge (German War Graves Commission), drew up plans considered to be typical of the National Socialist style: an entrance portal of archaising blocks gives onto a 'court of honour' flanked by four granite pillars topped with Roman-style fire pots. The cemetery is divided by a central alley leading to a monument made up of several ranks of five deep crosses aligned with individual graves on the sides. However, the outbreak of the Second World War put a definitive end to this proposal.

Within Ohlsdorf Cemetery is the Commonwealth Cemetery designed by Robert Lorimer (1864–1929) in 1926, according to Commonwealth War Graves Commission guidelines. Laid to rest are 676 prisoners of war and service personnel killed in action during the First World War, along with another 2,000 victims of the Second World War.

The 'memorial purges' that have succeeded one another with political crises have left their marks on Ohlsdorf, which is a veritable place of remembrance for the city of Hamburg. A monument to the fallen of the 1918–19 Revolution (inaugurated in 1922) was dismantled in 1933 by the Nazi authorities before being rehabilitated in 1945. Between 1933 and 1936 the Nazis built a 'court of honour' for their fallen. This entity was razed to the ground in 1945, with the exception of the crypts, which were overlooked.

Various monuments commemorate the Allied bombing campaigns on the city, particularly the horrific destruction of summer 1943. The monument for the victims of

Ohlsdorf Cemetery, Hamburg, *c.*2008

the Hamburg firestorm pays tribute to the 36,918 victims buried there. Antifascist sculptor Gerhard Marcks (1889–1981) designed the masterpiece (1952), a massive construction with tall walls that give a false impression of security, while in reality the monument lies open to the skies, recalling the state of the city after the bombings. A niche containing sculpted figures represents Marcks's interpretation of 'The passage over the River Styx'. The memorial was erected on the centre of a cross-shaped landscaped mass grave that contains the remains of the bodies gathered after the firestorm. The thick oak beams carved with the names of the various neighbourhoods of the dead date back to the Nazi era. The mass grave was supposed to represent the 'community of destiny' and in 1943 and 1944 it served as a place for communion and solidarity in adversity. After the war, the mass grave took on a more integrated meaning, symbolising both the annihilation and victim status of the civilians, but also the city's 'zero hour', a brand-new start.

Designed by Heinz Jürgen Ruscheweyh (1926–1978) and inaugurated in 1949, the memorial for the victims of Nazi persecution is a square, slightly concave, 15-storey tower that holds 105 ceramic urns containing the ashes of victims and the soil from 105 German concentration camps. The monument faces the former crematorium where victims of the regime were incinerated. The stone plinth that was supposed to link the two buildings together to underline the connection was never made.

In 1953 the German Second World War military cemetery was built and inaugurated on the spot where Cordes had planned to install a *Heldenhain* (heroes grove) in the natural style of the garden architect Willy Lange. After a short political quarantine, the Volksbund and Tischler were back in the forefront of cemetery design and proposed a central building. Reminiscent of such buildings made before the war, this memorial of honour is a compact antique rotunda with a heavy entablature and four columns. In a small space inside lies a sarcophagus slab. Having returned from exile, Gustav Oelsner (1879–1956) became the city architect and asked Robert Tischler to give his project a more classical form, creating inside it a figurative decor symbolising bereavement. Derided by some people, it is considered a 'temple of war' by the art historian Jörg Schilling. In any event, this memorial is typical of a transitional architecture, filled with compromise between yesteryear and a return to normalcy.

These examples testify to an incisive approach to memorialising. For instance, the rows of rustic crosses used by Tischler to mark the burial areas of the military necropolis cast their shadows on the graves of the many victims of the Nazi regime nearby. Some even consider this area to be a posthumous outrage to the victims.[2] In 2016 an association was created to reflect on an 'appropriate commemoration', perhaps even a 'counter-monument'. **B.K.**

1 Wilhelm Benque (1814–1895), a student of Peter Joseph Lenné (1789–1866), introduced the English garden model in Prussia. Exiled in 1849, he settled in New York, where he discovered 'rural cemeteries'. When he returned to Germany, he created Kiel's Südfriedhof (a landscape cemetery) and Bremen's municipal park.

2 Jörg Schilling, *Soldatengedenkhalle Friedhof Ohlsdorf* (*Hamburger Bauheft*, 17), Hamburg, 2016.

## Waldfriedhof, Munich (1907)

The term *Waldfriedhof* (woodland cemetery) predates the creation of this burial ground in Munich.[1] Like other parks, the Waldfriedhof was eulogised by poets and painted by artists before it was even completed.[2] Although German romantics revisited the 'wild' forest in order to create allegories of the 'beautiful and eternal life', this new vision did not circulate in the collective imagination before 1870. The new empire needed symbols in its quest for a single unity: the 'German forest' thus became the national incarnation of a fight for freedom and authenticity. Simultaneously, in the last years of the nineteenth century, galloping industrialisation and urbanisation provoked the emergence of a 'return to origins', where nature – and more specifically forest – played a crucial role.

In this context, Hans Grässel (1860–1939), architectural consultant for the city of Munich, designed a completely new cemetery genre, and dream became reality with the Waldfriedhof. Like most architects of his generation, he was bored with 'cemeteries without atmosphere, with endlessly aligned rows of tombs, devoid of greenery and filled with heterogeneous funeral monuments made out of disparate materials'. Like all big cities of the period, Munich required more space for its dead. Grässel had the idea to establish a new cemetery outside the city walls on a 160-hectare plot covered with a forest of conifers, where he would deliberately retain its sylvan aspect.

Grässel divided up the space into 240 sections, each with its own characteristics. The relative diversity was subject to ground rules: the size of headstones and monuments was determined; edges to the graves were forbidden, 'seeing that there are no limitations in a forest'; and the only materials allowed were natural stone and wood. Each funerary monument was subject to approval, and Grässel personally ensured that individual creations fitted in

Waldfriedhof, Munich, WW1 and WW2 (architect: Helmut Schöner-Fedrigotti; landscape design: Ludwig Roemer), 2019

with the general spirit of the Waldfriedhof, banishing any ostentation on principle. As with Hamburg's Ohlsdorf Cemetery, the different sections represented a variety of images that had to come together in a harmonious overall vista, combining the spectacle of natural life into one 'artistic vision'.[3]

Started in 1905, the works were finished in 1907, and very quickly Munich's Waldfriedhof became a model for other German cities. The *Waldfriedhof* concept and the word itself soon enjoyed great success. Many cemeteries that were improvised during the First World War would also be described in this way. Grässel did not escape the public debate about the form that these new burial grounds should take. In fact, he even contributed by elaborating assorted forms of headstones inspired by Bavarian popular art and regrouped in types, ensuring that shared destiny and military camaraderie were evident at first glance.

In 1960–64, the part of the cemetery where 2,000 soldiers had been laid to rest was replaced by a military necropolis regrouping 3,540 victims of both world wars – mostly soldiers, but also deported workers from many countries, and including women and children. The chief architect of the Volksbund Deutsche Kriegsgräberfürsorge (VDK; German War Graves Commission), Munich-born ethnicist and former Nazi, Robert Tischler (1885–1959), had died recently. As joint main contractor with the federal state, the VDK decided to entrust the completion of the landscaping of the new necropolis to architects Helmut Schöner-Fedrigotti and Ludwig Roemer.

The new complex was placed in a clearing surrounded by dense and dark groups of spruces. A high wall in natural stone leads visitors to an unsettling central monument. Resting on a black floor, a 13-metre-high quartz concrete triangle offers a play of light, projecting colours from its 1,800 cut crystals. A narrow window illuminates and colours the sculptures – which convey 'a concurrently chaotic and powerful movement'[4] – made up of 3,500 pieces of soldered metal, each engraved with the name of a soldier. The basin that must be crossed to reach the 'Island of the Dead' contributes to the originality of the work. Two white, colossal block crosses delineate the cemetery, which is punctuated by 3,520 square headstones in grey stone – the colour of the soldier's uniform – lying in the ground and each bearing an individual name. All the headstones were carved by students of the Academy of Fine Arts. Plants contrast with the solemn curtain of conifers, and in spring and autumn the site is covered with a delicate lilac veil of 3,500 crocus flowers. Around Pentecost, 10,000 *Hemerocallis* (daylilies) flower and die, symbolising the lives of the soldiers cut short. Emblematic of a generation of architects of the 1960s, the Munich war cemetery is a product of its time, with its triangular monument and its mirror of water borrowed from British and American garden cemeteries. Four years later, a similar triangular shape was constructed as part of the monument in the German War Cemetery in the Futa Pass, to the north of Florence. **B.K.**

---

1 It seems that the term first appeared in 1861 to designate the small cemetery where the founders of the Salzmannschule (Salzmann School) are buried, in Schnepfenthal, Thuringe. It reappears in 1876 concerning a plan relating to the spa garden of Mannheim, in southwestern Germany.

2 Notably by the poet Joseph von Eichendorff (1788–1857) and the painter Caspar David Friedrich (1774–1840).

3 Georg Jakob Wolf, *Münchener Waldfriedhof* (Augsburg: Benno Filser), 1928, p. 11.

4 *Die Kriegsgräberstätte München-Waldfriedhof*. Handwritten text to which we were kindly given access by Maximilian Fügen, Munich Volksbund.

## Cemeteries created by German soldiers in France, 1914–18

Summer 1914 proved to be gruesomely deadly. What was to be done with all these corpses lying in the summer heat? The 1906 Geneva Convention for the Amelioration of the Condition of Wounded, Sick and Shipwrecked Members of Armed Forces at Sea was silent on the burial of the dead. So, as always, the bodies were thrown in the mass graves of the battlefields.[1]

A monument and makeshift railing were added to this 1914 mass grave in Niderviller, Moselle. When he visited the nearby village of Dolving in August, where another communal grave for German and French soldiers had been dug, a Bavarian writer described the flowers growing there in lyrical terms: 'on the graves, the fire of rhododendron bushes is extinct, but in their place the rosebuds and blossoming pansies readily cover the ground'.[2]

But during September 1914 the front line gradually became more fixed. Troops faced one another and became immobilised. Soldiers stayed in the same billet for weeks, sometimes months. These soldiers were committed to making improvements to the commonplace wooden crosses: 'soldiers realised with great pride that these funeral monuments would sustain their glory. The most moving war cemeteries were created during a time when everyone could freely express their personality.'[3]

Soldiers were working as gardeners on the front line and a genuine sense of personal achievement materialised. At least, this is what is described in *Möllers Deutsche Gärtner-Zeitung*, the German horticulturists' journal: 'soldiers in khaki uniforms consider the planting and decoration of their comrades' tombs as an honourable commitment. Each tries to do better than the other; it is a veritable heroes' cemetery competition.'[4]

The shapes and forms of the headstones stand out against the improvised graveyards. The topography and military context are crucial. Very often, men have to remove the bodies from the trenches before burying them at night or while shielding themselves from the bombardments using whatever materials are

Mass grave, Niederweiler (Niderviller), 1914, postcard (undated)

available, such as stones gathered in the fields or branches found in neighbouring woods and forests.

The soldiers made death symbols that varied according to their regional customs, with popular art patterns rivalling military-inspired iconography. The German cemetery in Saint-Mihiel in the Meuse reflects this common disparity: wooden crosses are overwhelmed by creations in stone; a sculpted bas-relief rubs shoulders with an artillery shell, a relic of trench art. A rustic pathway leads to an elegant belvedere that overlooks the cemetery. As we have seen, the cemetery attracted a certain devotion, but it was also a place to pass the time: it was active while being maintained and contemplative when used for strolling. Some cemeteries were embellished with traced paths and edges, planted walls, resting benches, and were even visited by small groups, as was the case in Bouillonville for instance. Sometimes, small shrines offered shelter. Elsewhere, visitors might come across porticoes or ponds, as in the cemetery in Lagney in Meurthe-et-Moselle.

It is hardly surprising that this extreme display of patriotic energy and sometimes unbridled creativity should draw the attention of the military hierarchy. In July 1916 an administration was entrusted with keeping a record of the tombs. Burials and the regrouping of corpses took place according to a simple principle: 'the soldier should ideally be laid to rest where he fell for his motherland'.[5] The example came from above. Indeed, Kaiser Wilhelm II established a necropolis that remains virtually unchanged today: the Saint-Quentin French–German War Cemetery in the Aisne department. Designed according to prevailing academic principles and scattered with various Greek and Etruscan artistic references, this is the antithesis of the customary, self-built cemeteries. Inaugurated in the presence of the Kaiser on 18 October 1915, it was entrusted to the care of the city's authorities.

This is not the first time that Germany concerned itself with the aesthetics of cemeteries. At the turn of the twentieth century, a vast campaign was aimed at sustaining the unique characteristics of German nationhood in the context of an increasingly undifferentiated urban and industrialised society. This movement also affected funerary creations. Henceforth, the cemetery was to be designed as a whole, a unified collective work, not just a shapeless arrangement of headstones, a 'desert of stones'. However, the 'comrades' cemeteries' returned to the archaic old ways, devoid of style or unity, as at Saint-Mihiel for example. From spring 1916 onwards, ideas converged to define a more unitary and 'progressive' typology for the construction of war cemeteries. Renowned architects and sculptors contributed to this impassioned debate that related to identity and politics, and in 1917 the result of the work of these 'authorised voices' was published by the military authorities as a set of official guidelines.[6]

In actual fact, the Ministry of War and the Ministry of Cultural Affairs had sent a delegation of artists, architects and landscape gardeners to the Eastern Front to examine the situation and asked them to produce a form of building code, from which ten guiding principles emerged.[7] Their application was overseen by *Kunstbeiräte* (Art Advisers), who wore special uniforms and were to be consulted by the senior commanders of the different military zones. These principles were subject to various decrees of the Ministry of War before being confirmed by the Imperial Order of 28 February 1917, put into effect on 28 July.

It is impossible to determine the number of cemeteries affected by these new regulations during the short lapses of time between the major offensives of 1918, but the cemetery at Cambrai (Nord, France) deserves particular attention. Wilhelm Kreis (1873–1955), one of the Reich's leading architects, designed an ambitious scheme that, like at Saint-Quentin, welcomed both British and French 'heroes'.[8] It was inaugurated on 11 August 1918, three days after what General Ludendorff would call 'the darkest day of the German Army'. The Hundred Days Offensive (the last series of Allied victories before the Armistice of 11 November 1918) proved to be a turning point for the German soldiers' cemeteries. Many, which were deemed unfinished,

German war cemeteries:

Bétheniville, Marne, postcard, 1915

Bois Brûlé, near Verdun, Meuse, postcard, July 1915

Saint-Mihiel, Meuse, postcard, undated

Sainte-Marie-aux-Mines, Haut-Rhin, postcard, 1916–17, and current state

were destroyed during the course of the fighting and by desecrations voluntarily committed by inhabitants. Berlin architect and Second Lieutenant Wilhelm Keller spoke of an 'intermediate state'. While the French were regaining control over their territory, what was to become of these creations in which so many passions and hopes had been invested? **B.K.**

1 Olivier Monier, 'Quand les canons se sont tus: Le traitement des corps des soldats tombés au cours de la bataille de Sarrebourg (20 août 1914)', *Revue d'Alsace* 139 (2013), pp. 291–304.

2 Josef M. Jurinek, *Bayernsiege und Heldengräber: Die Lothringer Schlacht am 19./20. August 1914* (Munich/Berlin: Drei-Masken-Verlag), 1915.

3 Rudolf Schumacher, 'Fürsorge für die Gefallenen und die Kriegergräber', in Hans von Winterfeld (ed.), *Die Organisation der Kriegsführung: Der Große Krieg 1914–1918: Die Organisationen für das gestige Leben im Heere. Dritter Teil*, Leipzig, 1923, pp. 328–47, here p. 330.

4 *Möllers Deutsche Gärtner-Zeitung* (October 1915).

5 K. H. Schäfer, 'Die Soldatengräberfürsorge im Weltkrieg', *Kriegsgräberfürsorge* 8/6 (June 1928), p. 333.

6 *Kriegsgräber im Felde und daheim: Herausgegeben im Einvernehmen mit der Heeresverwaltung* (Munich: Bruckmann), 1917.

7 The instruction manual, including illustrations, can be viewed at <https://digital.staatsbibliothek-berlinde7289793 57&PHYSID=PHYS_0026&DMDID=DMDLOG_0001.>

8 Kreis was possibly the most influential architect of his era. In 1941 the Nazi regime appointed him head of the Generalbaurat für die Gestaltung der Deutschen Kriegerfriedhöfe (General Building Council for the Design of German War Cemeteries).

## Skogskyrkogården, Stockholm

In 1915 the Stockholm municipality launched an international competition for the design of a new cemetery in the southern part of the city on former quarries overgrown with pine trees. The Skogskyrkogården – The Woodland Cemetery – can be seen as belonging to a context that included burial reform brought about by the invention of modern cremation in 1872 and the woodland cemeteries movement of Germany and Switzerland. In Sweden, the enthusiasm for this type of cemetery stemmed from the nostalgia for a woodland of pine and spruce trees, characteristic of Nordic landscapes.

For urban citizens, this new type of cemetery was also a means of reviving sensations that had all but disappeared in cities, while also re-establishing connections with the pagan roots of forest people. The fame of German woodland cemeteries such as Hamburg's Ohlsdorf Cemetery and Munich's Waldfriedhof further encouraged the municipality to integrate German design into the formulation of the programme, giving the competition an international dimension.

Several of the competition proposals assimilated these ideas, particularly Gunnar Asplund's and Sigurd Lewerentz's winning 'Tallum' project, which blended a modern interpretation of landscape with an architecture that encompassed all elements, from a general plan down to the tiniest details of lighting and furniture. Lewerentz designed the overall layout, the main entrance and the Chapel of Resurrection (1921–5), while Asplund concentrated on other constructions, including the Woodland Chapel (1918–21), inspired by a simple cottage in the park at Liselund (island of Møn, Denmark), and the Woodland Crematorium (1935–40).

According to Asplund, 'the character and dimensions of the landscape could not have accommodated a larger, more compact edifice. Monumentality is traditionally intended for biblical landscapes.' One huge solitary granite cross (designed by Asplund in 1939) dominates the open landscape. Inspired by Caspar David Friedrich's, it is open to non-faith interpretations. Citing Friedrich, Asplund and Lewerentz noted that it could be seen simply as a cross as much as a symbol of consolation. The complex appears like an innovative and remarkable interpretation of the spiritual landscape, where particular attention has been given to the planting and the architecture placed along paths bordered by low headstones.[1] In 1994, Skogskyrkogården was added to the UNESCO World Heritage List.[2] **M.R.**

1 The influence of Skogskyrkogården on military cemetery design of both world wars deserves to be documented, but the British and German architects who were creating their own projects at the end of the First World War were undoubtedly familiar with the Stockholm scheme.

2 See <whc.unesco.org/en/list/558>.

Skogskyrkogården (The Woodland Cemetery), Stockholm, 1917–20 (architects: Gunnar Asplund and Sigurd Lewerentz): meditation hill

## The VDK's design of military cemeteries

### The foundation of the VDK and its initial years of activity

The end of the First World War saw the downfall of the German Empire. When structures were newly established in 1919, the maintenance of war graves fell to state institutions. In addition to their organisation, another challenge was how to finance them, which seemed almost impossible in view of current inflation. Thus, when the Volksbund Deutsche Kriegsgräberfürsorge (VDK; German War Graves Commission), a private association, appeared as a non-governmental organisation and a financially independent sponsor alongside the state institutions in 1919, their interest was much welcomed.[1] In fact, the VDK's predominant task during its early years of existence was to obtain information about the location and condition of military graves, or to have them decorated by foreign helpers.

*Totenburg*, Bitola, Macedonia, 1934 (architect: Robert Tischler)

### The mid-1920s: the design of military cemeteries

Prepared by the official German authorities, an agreement was reached with France in 1926, so that the VDK became able to take an active role in planning. Landscape architect Robert Tischler, employed by the VDK in 1926, was largely responsible for the design of the sites.[2] As a 'non-governmental' organisation – and also because it participated in the instigated measures with financial donations – the VDK was granted a number of rights. Its main area of activity was in France and parts of Belgium. Most of the cemeteries there had already been laid out by the Germans during the First World War. In mergers carried out between 1922 and 1924, the French had reduced the number of cemeteries from about 4,000 predominantly smaller ones to around 210, including 70 new French creations – among them, Saint-Vaast (La Maison Blanche) with about 40,000 and Saint-Laurent-Blangy with about 22,000 individual graves. The barrenness of these gigantic collective cemeteries in France was shattering in its impact, reinforced because no planting broke up the endless black sea of grave crosses. In addition, large mass graves had arisen in many of the cemeteries, since it was no longer possible for the French to assign the names of the fallen to individual plots after the reburials.[3]

Initially, the design of the cemeteries followed ideas that had already been developed during the First World War. This was especially true in respect to the use of trees. Here, the VDK was not restricted to specific tree species and often adapted planting to the woods of the surrounding landscape. In addition to their space-creating components, such memorial groves in particular became typical of VDK sites. In mainly laying out the groves by the mass graves, Tischler's designs made these parts of the cemeteries more prominent. The importance of the groves derived not only from design factors but also from their longevity and the symbolic power of the 'Holy Grove', which elevated the cemeteries into sacred places. The designs related closely to the surrounding landscape, so that they were incorporated into it – by means of visual references, for instance – but they remained very restrained, lending the sites a supposedly typical German character.[4]

Trees and plants were employed to veil the finality of death.[5] The VDK dispensed with lavish flower arrangements in favour of perennials, which were both robust and easy to care for. Evergreen, heather, wild roses and lavender (and more rarely lilies) as well as grass, clover and wildflower mixtures were planted. This softened the harsh, barren character of the grave fields while keeping the design simple and intentionally natural. Large, tall crosses, which due to their size dominated the cemeteries, had also been adopted from the First World War sites.

### The 1930s: the Volksbund develops its own formal language

The identification of individual graves was abandoned increasingly in favour of an all-encompassing comradeship of the dead, emphasising the national sacrifice. The VDK initially created groups of symbolic crosses on enclosed areas of heather or lawns with a central memorial. These crosses did not bear names, since they did not indicate the exact burial place of a fallen soldier. The names of the dead were written, for example, in a memorial book, on commemorative plaques, wall inscriptions or communal gravestones. Regarding the collective graves, the VDK spoke for the first time of a 'field of honour' in the cemetery. The groves were retained, but the embellishment of the cemeteries with architectural components – such as gate buildings, memorial monuments or edging with sturdy walls – became more obvious. The VDK deliberately focused on traditional trade techniques and tried to use local building materials in its cemeteries.[6] In this context, planting was reduced, and plants thereby lost their significance as primary design elements.

Access to the cemetery was usually through an entry so narrow that one could only pass through it one by one. These staged gate buildings functioned like guard houses but also as sanctified areas. Before the sea of graves was revealed to the visitor, their passage was blocked by a new wall or tall hedge. Thus an anteroom was created, intended for collection and reflection, and often provided with an inscription. Only after proceeding through this anteroom did one enter the actual cemetery, the 'space of silence'.[7] The mighty walls and buildings were reminders of a 'European fortress architecture', its symbolic fortifications even seeming to suggest that the war had not yet ended.[8]

The culmination of this development – so to speak – was the concept introduced by Tischler at the end of the 1920s: the so-called *Totenburgen* (fortresses of the dead), the first of which was to be established by the Volksbund at Bitola in 1934.[9] These produced the effect of defiant forts and were reminiscent of bunkers or medieval ramparts. While, due to their monumentality, the castles were a kind of fortification on the outside, inside they were sacred memorials. This was achieved with the use of statues of mourning soldiers and sculptures, candlelight and fire bowls, skilful use of light and, for instance, altar-like memorial monuments.[10]

### The VDK's work during and after the Second World War

The outbreak of war meant that the Wehrmacht took over the maintenance of graves, which also included the burial and registration of the fallen.[11] The only remaining task for the VDK was the expansion of its burial castles and some of the military cemeteries from the First World War.

After the war ended, the VDK was recognised by the British (1946) and the USA (1947) as an institution responsible for the care of war graves.[12] Numerous authors have pointed out the VDK's lack of reflection in its approach to its own history during the National Socialist period. For example, many of the VDK's employees continued to work for the Commission immediately after the war, which brought continuity but clearly stood in the way of a true new beginning. It is not surprising, therefore, that designs tended to adhere to the same criteria and continued to comprise heroic groves and fortresses of the dead, thus creating sites – even after the end of the war – which eloquently expressed a profoundly national sentiment.[13]

It was only after Tischler's death in 1959 that the VDK altered the appearance of its sites, by, for example, putting up name crosses again and concentrating on memorial buildings such as chapels or monuments that were less fortified than they had been previously. What remained, however, was the sites' uniform design: clearly indicating that here soldiers were resting in regimented rows under a shared covering of lawn, not yet discharged from their duty by death.[14] **S.R.**

Entrance, *Totenburg*, Bitola, Macedonia, 1934 (architect: Robert Tischler)

1 Funds belonging to a private association could not be confiscated for reparation payments.

2 Gert Gröning and Joachim Wolschke-Bulmahn, *Grüne Biographien: Biographisches Handbuch zur Landschaftsarchitektur des 20. Jahrhunderts in Deutschland* (Berlin/Hanover: Patzer), 1997, p. 389; Christian Fuhrmeister, 'Der Volksbund Deutsche Kriegsgräberfürsorge im 20. und 21. Jahrhundert: Bemerkungen aus Sicht der politischen Ikonographie', in Ellen Ueberschär (ed.), *Soldaten und andere Opfer? Die Täter-Opfer-Problematik in der deutschen Erinnerungskultur und das Gedenken an die Opfer von Krieg und Gewaltherrschaft* (Documentation of a conference at the Evangelische Akademie Loccum,

9–11 December 2005) (Rehburg-Loccum: Evangelische Akad.), 2007, pp. 45–67, here pp. 48–9; Simon Rietz, *Deutsche Soldatenfriedhöfe des Ersten Weltkrieges und der Weimarer Republik: Ein Beitrag zur Professionsgeschichte der Landschaftsarchitektur*, PhD dissertation, Gottfried Wilhelm Leibniz Universität, Hanover, 2015 <http://edok01.tib.uni-hannover.de/edoks/e01dh15/841205302.pdf>, pp. 440–41. For more on Tischler, see Christian Fuhrmeister, 'Robert Tischler, Chefarchitekt 1926–1959: Ein Desiderat', *RIHA Journal* 0159 (27 June 2017) <RIHA_Journal_0159_Fuhrmeister.odt.pdf>.

3 Of the approximately 900,000 fallen German soldiers who lay buried in France at the end of the war, only about half could still be identified by name after the French exhumations and reburials (Meinhold Lurz, *Kriegerdenkmäler in Deutschland*, vol. 4., *Weimarer Republik* [Heidelberg: Esprint-Verlag], 1985, p. 124). Klaus von Lutzau starts out from the assumption that 160,000 German soldiers were 'lost' throughout the course of the reburials (Klaus von Lutzau, '40 Jahre Volksbund Deutsche Kriegsgräberfürsorge', in Volksbund Deutsche Kriegsgräberfürsorge [ed.], *40 Jahre Volksbund Deutsche Kriegsgräberfürsorge*, Neuwied, 1959, pp. 5–59, here pp. 18ff).

4 Christian Fuhrmeister, 'Klatschmohn und Ochsenblut: Zur Ikonographie der Kriegsgräberstätten des Volksbundes Deutsche Kriegsgräberfürsorge', in Gert Gröning and Uwe Schneider (eds), *Gartenkultur und nationale Identität: Strategien nationaler und regionaler Identitätsstiftung in der deutschen Gartenkultur. Grüne Reihe* (Worms: Wernersche Verlagsgesellschaft), 2001, vol. 22, pp. 119–34, here p. 129.

5 The allegory inherent in plant growth – that is, its apparent death in autumn and resurgence in spring – could be interpreted as a symbol of rebirth. This motif played a key part in the design of military cemeteries (George L. Mosse, *Fallen Soldiers: Reshaping the Memory of the World Wars* [New York: Oxford University Press], 1990, p. 153; Fuhrmeister 2001, op. cit., p. 125; Anette Freytag and Thomas Van Driessche, 'Die Deutschen Soldatenfriedhöfe des Ersten Weltkriegs in Flandern', *Relicta: Archeologie, Monumenten- en Landschapsonderzoek in Vlaandern* 7 [2011], pp. 163–238, here p. 17[illegible]; Rietz, op. cit., pp. 486ff). For more on the universal appropriation of nature in landscape architecture, see Joachim Wolschke-Bulmahn, *Auf der Suche nach Arkadien: Zu Landschaftsidealen und Formen der Naturaneignung der Jugendbewegung und ihrer Bedeutung für die Landespflege*, doctoral dissertation, Berlin University of the Arts, 1990.

6 Numerous articles by Hans Gstettner in the VDK members' journal from 1939 to 1942 can be seen as exemplary in this context. Even after the Second World War, this approach was recommended explicitly by the VDK (Volksbund Deutsche Kriegsgräberfürsorge [ed.], *Gestaltung von Kriegsgräberstätten: Hinweise und Richtlinien*, Kassel, 1954). An overview is provided by Fuhrmeister 2001, op. cit.

7 Max Arendt, 'Die Bauten des Volksbundes in ihrer geschichtlichen und kulturellen Bedeutung', *Kriegsgräberfürsorge* 2 (1935), pp. 19–24, here p. 20. Langemark Cemetery (planned 1929, dedicated 1932) is exemplary of such a scheme. This has been examined by various authors, also due to its significance for the 'nationalisation' of the war dead.

8 Fuhrmeister 2007, op. cit., p. 54.

9 The earliest plan for a *Totenburg* was in Bitola on the Yugoslav–Greek border, begun by Tischler in 1929/30. It was projected for the first time in 1932, built as from 1934, and dedicated in 1936. For more about this, see Franz Hallbaum, 'Die Totenburg deutscher Helden in Bitolij, Jugoslawien', in *Kriegsgräberfürsorge* 16 (1936), p. 11; or the evaluation by Christian Fuhrmeister, 'Die "unsterbliche Landschaft", der Raum des Reiches und die Toten der Nation – Die Totenburgen Bitoli (1936) und Quero (1939) als strategische Memorialarchitektur', *Kritische berichte: Mitteilungsorgan des Ulmer Vereins – Verband für Kunst- und Kulturwissenschaften e.V* 29/2 (2001), pp. 56–70.

10 Meinhold Lurz, '"... ein Stück Heimat in fremder Erde": Die Heldenhaine und Totenburgen des Volksbunds Deutsche Kriegsgräberfürsorge', *Arch+: Zeitschrift für Architektur und Städtebau* 71 (1983), pp. 66–70, here p. 68; Monika Kuberek, 'Die Kriegsgräberstätten des Volksbundes Deutsche Kriegsgräberfürsorge', in Michael Hütt et al., *Unglücklich das Land, das Helden nötig hat: Leiden und Sterben in den Kriegsdenkmälern des Ersten und Zweiten Weltkriegs (Studien zur Kunst- und Kulturgeschichte*, vol. 8) (Marburg: Jonas Verlag), 1990, pp. 75–90, here p. 83. On the occasion of the 75th anniversary of the opening of the Quero 'fortress of the dead' in 2014, the VDK published a small brochure about the site, which conveys an excellent impression, partly due to its wise choice of illustrations: Volksbund Deutsche Kriegsgräberfürsorge (ed.): *Eine Festung, die ein Friedhof ist: In Stein gefasste Ideologie – 75 Jahre Totenburg Quero*, 2014 <https://www.volksbund.de/fileadmin/redaktion/BereichMeldungen/Presse/2014/Prospekt_Quero.pdf>.

11 On this, see Nina Janz's proposed doctoral dissertation, 'Ehrenhaine und Heldengräber – Friedhöfe und Kriegsgräber des Zweiten Weltkrieges als raumgebundene Topographie deutschen Heldentums 1939–1945' and Nina Janz, *'Totenhügel und Waldfriedhöfe* – die Gräber und Friedhöfe für gefallene Wehrmachtssoldaten während des Zweiten Weltkriegs zwischen individueller Gräberfürsorge und nationalsozialistischem Totenkult', *RIHA Journal* 0174 (27 June 2017) <http://www.riha-journal.org/articles/2017/0150-0176-special-issue-war-graves/0174-janz)>.

12 Archive of the federal office of the Volksbund Deutsche Kriegsgräberfürsorge Kassel, 'VKA A.10-24 Arbeitsgenehmigung in der Westzone 1946–1949', as quoted in J. Böttcher, *Zwischen staatlichem Auftrag und gesellschaftlicher Trägerschaft : Eine Geschichte der Kriegsgräberfürsorge in Deutschland im 20. Jahrhundert. Studien zur Zivilgesellschaft* (Manfred Hettling and Paul Nolte, ed.), vol. 17, 2018.

13 For example, the *Totenburgen* memorials in Tobruk, Libya (1954–5) and El Alamein, Egypt (1956–9) were built after the war. On this, see Kai Kappel, 'Die Totenburgen von Tobruk und El Alamein – strategische Memorialarchitektur für die Bundesrepublik', *RIHA Journal* 0161 (27 June 2017) <http://www.riha-journal.org/articles/2017/0150-0176-special-issue-war-graves/0161-kappel>.

14 Marking the VDK's 100th anniversary, Christian Fuhrmeister is currently working on an investigation into the War Graves Commission within the context of a research project: Christian Fuhrmeister, *Dauerndes Ruherecht und nationale Erinnerungsdynamik: Der 'Volksbund Deutsche Kriegsgräberfürsorge e.V.' 1919–2019* (forthcoming).

German War Cemetery, La Maison Blanche, Neuville-Saint-Vaast, Pas-de-Calais, postcard issued in 1930

Brieulles-sur-Meuse German War Cemetery, extended by the VDK in 1931–6

## Four German architects

### Willy Lange (1864–1941) and the *Heldenhaine* (1915)

As a designer of an 'ecological aesthetic', Willy Lange championed natural garden design before the term 'ecology' was popular. Considered one of the precursors of eugenics and National Socialist ideology, he felt that the German people enjoyed a genetically based relationship with nature. In 1915 he gained sudden fame with his national campaign for a new style of memorial: the *Heldenhaine* (groves of heroes), where an oak tree was planted to represent each fallen soldier. In the middle of this oak grove stood a linden tree, representing peace. This place would be used for mourning and for community gatherings, and would also serve as the setting for entertainment or sport activities. However, it quickly became all too clear that Lange's project was unrealistic, due to the growing number of dead soldiers and therefore of trees.

Yet the word and the concept remained – and some *Heldenhaine* were completed, notably during the 1920s. However, most were heavily criticised before being dismantled and renamed – after 1990 – as *Friedenshaine* (groves of peace).

### Wilhelm Kreis (1873–1955) and the Memorial to the Dead of the Reich project (1931)

Germany's most important architect of memorials during the twentieth century was undeniably Wilhelm Kreis. In 1813, while still a student, he won a competition to design the Monument to the Battle of the Nations (dedicated to the Battle of Leipzig). In 1899 he once again grabbed attention when he won a national competition to celebrate Bismarck, who had died the previous year. His archaising tower design, inspired by Wagner's *Twilight of the Gods*, was to be a huge success, becoming a standard form repeated 47 times throughout the Reich (578 times including variants).

During the First World War, there are traces of his work in the Evere district of Brussels, where he designed the war cemetery and its classical temple – a modest, airy and simple cube (1917). During the Weimar Republic, Kreis participated in the competition for a Memorial to the Dead of the Reich, but the project was later abandoned by Hitler. Its massive style was a forerunner of the grandiloquent forms of the 1930s, and combined modern simplicity and pseudo-Teutonic nostalgia.

In 1941, Hitler appointed Kreis as head of the Generalbaurat für die Gestaltung der Deutschen Kriegerfriedhöfe (General Building Council for the Design of German War Cemeteries). Kreis's sketches for his projects, which were to extend across the four corners of Nazi-occupied Europe, never saw the light of day, since Hitler envisaged completing them after the 'Ultimate Victory'.

### Ernst May (1886–1970)

Responsible for the New Frankfurt large-scale public housing programme (1925–9) during the Weimar Republic, Ernst May became known for his functional, airy and affordable solutions. During the First World War, he had shown great enthusiasm in designing war cemeteries, his sketchbooks testifying to an avant-garde imagination: a building topped with a Memorial Linden Tree reflected in a pond; a tiered pyramid of wooden terraces crowned with an immense antique dome of fire, entitled the 'Temple of the Atheists'. Finally, an unlikely common grave for his comrades: stakes planted side by side in the earth to form a defensive circle, each stake topped off with a *Pickelhaube*, the spiked helmet worn by the German military. Although these drawings did not convince the military authorities to appoint May as Inspector of War Graves in 1917, they were seduced by his concrete and more conventional projects in France, Romania, Poland and Lithuania. The only unusual creation to materialise was in Romania, where the uprights of crosses were replaced with spears.

### Dieter Oesterlen (1911–1994)

One of the architects who left a deeper impression on post-1945 German reconstruction, Dieter Oesterlen created two war cemeteries for the Volksbund Deutsche Kriegsgräberfürsorge (German War Graves Commission): the Futa Pass Cemetery (Italy's largest war cemetery, situated between Florence and Bologna) and the Bordj Cedria German War Cemetery, south-east of Tunis (1973–5). Both projects can be viewed as architectural landscapes that broke with the aesthetics of Robert Tischler, who had died in 1959.

For the design of the Futa Pass Cemetery in 1959, Oesterlen worked with three landscape architects, including Berlin-born Walter Rossow (1910–1992) and sculptor Helmut Langer (1924–2013), who were both former Nazi opponents – an emblematic choice. The site is marked out by a long

Wilhelm Kreis's preparatory drawing for the Memorial to the Dead of the Reich (1931), Bad Berka, Thuringia, to be at the heart of a 'forest of honour' spread over several thousand hectares

'Common grave for the comrades', where the stelae of the crosses are replaced with spears, Romania, *c.*1916 (architect: Ernst May)

wall that spirals around the hillside, starting rather insignificantly and accompanying the visitor to the cemetery's different burial sections set out on lawns. A stone terrace stands at the end of the 2-kilometre wall, which continues its spiral trajectory and rises to culminate in a 16-metre-tall jagged peak before dropping abruptly – in what Oesterlen planned as a critical allegory of the death of the soldiers.

This very realistic, even brutal, gesture was a break with traditional Christian architectural language that soothed but in transcending feelings perhaps dissimulated them. At the same time, this edifice can also be perceived as the expression of a self-confident Germany proud of its 'economic miracle'. Through its angular forms and broken lines, the cemetery can also be considered as a manifesto of adhesion to the expressionism of the Weimar Republic. It would seem that Oesterlen drew his inspiration from Walter Gropius's Monument to the March Dead (1920–22), which was built to honour workers killed in the Kapp Putsch. This memorial was destroyed by the Nazis in 1936 but reconstructed immediately after the war. **B.K.**

## The simplicity of the French National Cemeteries

The simplicity of most French cemeteries contrasts with the landscape and architectural style of Allied and German cemeteries. Indeed, at the end of the First World War, France emerged from the conflict, bled dry, humanly and financially, and shaken socially. All the same, like all other countries, the nation wanted to grant individual graves to each of its fallen soldiers and civilians, and to honour the memory of its dead. It differed from other countries by the rarity of named memorials on funeral sites, which were replaced with communal war memorials.

The task was colossal. Apart from having to bury a million bodies, France also supervised the burials of German soldiers in collaboration with the Volksbund Deutsche Kriegsgräberfürsorge (German War Graves Commission), a humanitarian organisation founded on 16 December 1919. Time was running short, the rehabilitation of the battlefield sites was urgent and the lack of financial means justified limited clean-up operations – the absence of proper architectural design, the choice of concrete (a cheap material) and standard formulaic plans for the new memorials, the National Cemeteries. Among the hundreds of cemeteries created during the conflict, only 275 cemeteries and 2,200 military plots within civilian graveyards were maintained and/or reconstructed and/or created by the state on the front line. Nowadays the national ceremonies are managed by the Direction des Patrimoines, de la Mémoire et des Archives (DPMA; Directorate of Heritage, Memory and Archives), under the auspices of the French Ministry of Defence, with the support of the Office National des Anciens Combattants et Victimes de Guerre (ONACVG; National Office for Veterans and Victims of War).

Every soldier was entitled to an individual grave, a democratic principle of modern society linked to the evolution of burial methods in civil society. For the first time in modern history, the new military memorial became national. During the American Civil War, it was reserved for the soldiers of the Union and, exceptionally, Confederate fighters. When the French entered the First World War, the regulations in force still stipulated mass graves for ordinary soldiers. But this rule became outdated by actual practices, soldiers spontaneously giving their comrades individual burials when they could, while also trying to preserve their identities. The army was thus forced to adjust its directives. A decree of the Grand Quartier Général (the general headquarters of the French Army) dated 22 February 1915 recommended burial in individual graves in principle, while still mentioning mass graves. The law of 29 December 1915 affirmed that 'any soldier who has died for France has the right to a grave in perpetuity at the expense of the state', which was also to be applied to the dead previously buried in mass graves.

National cemetery of Rethel, Ardennes, WW1 and WW2

The French military cemetery is recognisable by its alignment of tombs and headstones, similar to that of a regiment ready for battle. Sometimes, harking back to a Bavarian tradition, generals were buried in the middle of their troops, as in the Espérance National Cemetery in Cutting, Moselle.[1] The law did not define the exact architectural design, however, and so these cemeteries each have their own particularities. Thousands of military plots were filled with the bodies of the wounded who had died in hospitals and ambulances. Not everyone possessed an individual grave. Some bodies had no name, other bodies had disappeared altogether and could only be remembered with a memorial, meaning that a monument erected on the funeral ground rarely included names (National Cemetery, Leintrey).[2] Most often, communal war memorials fulfilled this role in France.[3] No ossuary, including those at Douaumont, Navarin and Notre-Dame-de-Lorette, made specific mention of each name. The law of 25 October 1919 concerning the commemoration and glorification of those who had died for France was still not completely enforced.[4] France met only the most urgent needs.

The law of 29 December 1915 established a simplified procedure of public pronouncement for the purchase of plots, each grave to be allocated 3 square metres. Supervised by the Ministry of Pensions, the Construction Department was charged with the purchase and building of plots but had no real architectural remit. Its mission consisted in 'choosing the locations, the land, organising the purchase, drawing up the boundaries for the cemeteries, enclosing them and making them fit to host bodies'.[5] The National Commission for Military Graves was set up in November 1918, after the Armistice. Paul Doumer, who had lost his four sons, and General Édouard de Curières de Castelnau, who had lost three, defended the burial of all fallen soldiers in military cemeteries, 'following the example of the admirable Meuse-Argonne American Cemetery'.[6] The Finance Law of 31 July 1920 prescribed that 'war cemeteries that have been created or that will be created to host the ashes of the fallen of the Great War are deemed national property and are preserved and maintained at the Nation's expense'. Moreover, widows, parents and children were also entitled to the restitution and transfer of the body of their dead relative at the state's expense. Article 8 of the same law established the terms of the financial allocation and, finally, 250,000 bodies were given back to their families. The law of 21 October 1921 granted the families the right to an annual visit to their relative's grave paid for by the state. Certain burial grounds, such as Fleury-devant-Douaumont, had their own pilgrimage house or visitors' centre. This partial restitution of bodies set apart French cemeteries where 730,000 fallen rest from Commonwealth cemeteries and their monuments, and matches them with American and German cemeteries. These places of remembrance do not represent the entire sacrificed nation.[7]

Unlike the funeral design of some German sites and that of the other Allies, French projects did not involve any architectural or landscape design research but was purely functional. If there were any specific characteristics, they came about via external influences and were financed by donations. In 1926 the state commissioned and financed a monument by the renowned sculptor Paul Landowski (1875–1961), called *La France en Marche* and also known as *Les Fantômes* (The Ghosts).[8] The figurative memorial was erected on the Butte Chalmont (near Oulchy-le-Château, Aisne) to commemorate the fallen of 1918 during the Second Battle of the Marne.

While the first regrouping of bodies started in November 1918[9] on confirmed sites such as the Riche National Cemetery, a major remembrance place for Saint-Cyr servicemen,[10] one of the first graveyards to be designed was the Sarrebourg National Cemetery for Prisoners of War.[11] In 1921, regardless of Article 226 of the Treaty of Versailles obliging the German government to properly maintain the graves of prisoners of war and interned civilians of the different belligerent states who had died in captivity in Germany, the German Minister of War and of Pensions decided to return claimed bodies to their relatives and to repatriate the other bodies to French territory. On 2 June 1922, André Maginot, Minister of War and of Pensions, ratified the creation of the so-called Hasenweide Cemetery near Oberwald (Switzerland), the view towards the blue-tinged tops of the Vosges mountains being the deciding factor. This symbolic location, a former artillery platform, was passed on to the Engineering Department as a gift and was arranged according to a very simple plan. The multiconfessional site gathered together 65 nationalities: headstones were erected for Christians, Muslims, freethinkers, Jews and other civilians of all ages. Based on a very simple symmetrical layout, all 13,326 graves were distributed according to a strict geometric pattern, on both sides of a central 9-metre-wide pathway leading to the ossuaries situated on opposite sides of a square esplanade, like a parade ground. On this was erected *Le Géant enchaîné*, a statue by Freddy Stoll (1869–1949), himself a former prisoner of war. Bodies were buried according to their order of arrival from the German cemeteries and equality before death was respected. At a slight remove from the other plots is the Muslim section with its characteristic arched headstones. The best example of a practice that was common to many front-line cemeteries – that of dedicated military or national plots – can be found in the Chambière National Cemetery, Metz.[12] The Prisoners of War Cemetery was among the first to replace its wooden crosses and other emblems with concrete headstones.

The architecture of Sarrebourg responded to the rules for the period's cemeteries without fully complying with a predefined standardised layout, which was not imposed until the Circular of 24 February 1927.[13] Funds raised by subscription allowed the planting of the cemetery, despite the rules about standardisation, a law that was to provoke heated reactions and that ended the planting of flowers, leaving place for bare lawns.[14] The wooden or stone emblems such as those found in the nonconfessional cemetery at Lagarde (Moselle) made room for concrete headstones.[15]

The Sarrebourg model was used for all the major regrouping cemeteries of the post-war period. This was the case in La Crouée, Souain-Perthes-lès-Hurlus (Battle of the Hills in 1917), where 30,732 French soldiers were laid to rest in an area spread over 60,384 square metres, in 9,034 individual graves and eight ossuaries housing 21,688 bodies, 8,498 of which were soldiers.[16] In La Targette, Neuville-Saint-Vaast (Pas-de-Calais), lie at rest 11,443 killed during the First and Second Battles of Artois, including the remains of 3,382 unidentified soldiers gathered in two ossuaries.[17] Even in larger cemeteries, ossuaries were limited in size. Created in 1923, the National Cemetery at Fleury-devant-Douaumont regrouped 16,142 graves, in addition to a 16-hectare ossuary that housed the remains of 130,000 French and German soldiers.[18] The Notre-Dame-de-Lorette National Cemetery (also known as the Ablain-Saint-Nazaire French War Cemetery) is a 13-hectare rectangular site that includes 19,510 graves and 20,000 remains placed in ossuaries.[19] Unlike most other National Cemeteries, however, this one displays an attempt at integration with the landscape. It is protected on each side by a hedge and trees, but its plan remains traditional: two perpendicular paths divide the cemetery into four sections, where graves are aligned in continuous rows. The graves of Jewish and Muslim soldiers were regrouped in the cemetery's southwestern section. The site spreads out over an area of 30.5 hectares, making it the world's largest French military cemetery. Such density of graves contrasts with the layout of the Meuse-Argonne American Cemetery and Memorial, where 14,246 burial plots are separated into eight rectangular sections on the north slope of a hill at the heart of a park criss-crossed by majestic avenues, all of which stretches over an area of 37.42 hectares.[20]

Dictated by economic considerations, these choices prompted the irritation of members

'Les Entonnoirs' French National Cemetery, Leintrey, Meurthe-et-Moselle (craters, 10 July 1916)

of the military world, who were shocked by the comparison with the memorials of Britain's Imperial War Graves Commission (IWGC).[21] The French state was forced to refuse some building permits, to request that the IWGC simplify the Loos Memorial (to British and Commonwealth soldiers) and the Pozières Memorial (to British soldiers), and to construct a memorial wall. However, building permission for the overwhelmingly monumental Thiepval Memorial to the Missing of the Somme was only granted on condition that it was dedicated to both the French and the English, and that a multiconfessional cemetery was created at its base.[22]

Some cemeteries that were created by the soldiers during the war and that have remained at their original sites reflect unique characteristics. Such is the case for the craters (Les Entonnoirs) in the cemetery at Leintrey, which was recognised as a National Cemetery after a marathon legal battle by the families of the dead, who wanted to erect a monument. In contrast, the site of the French–German Petit Donon cemetery, the most remarkable on this front, was not granted this privilege.

Local populations sometimes carried out burials and created variations of the cemetery on their own initiative, both alone and in collaboration with the French Army. In Reillon and other places in Meurthe-et-Moselle, schoolteachers and volunteers buried the dead in the zone that had fallen back under French control. In Friscati, near Lunéville (also in Meurthe-et-Moselle), schoolteacher Marie-Marguerite Wibrotte purchased a 10,555 square metre plot of land in Le Mouton Noir locality in order to create a cemetery.[23] During the First Battle of the Marne, inhabitants in Villeroy buried the dead in a beetroot pit.[24] Local personalities often worked hand in hand with the French Army in order to adapt their plans to the locations. Souain's L'Opéra National Cemetery, dear to the novelist Blaise Cendrars, was created by families who regularly planted the tombs with flowers. In time, shrubbery bordered the graves and a running brook appeared.[25]

In order to pay homage to the fallen who had died for their motherland, the German Army created some cemeteries behind the front and sometimes on the front line itself. The Bavarian proverb 'Enemies in life, friends in death' was used as an epitaph on many Calvary crosses and shared memorials erected during the conflict. During the fiasco of August 1914, the French Army was forced to abandon its fallen. The German Army instantly created cemeteries in the occupied zone with the help of local inhabitants and schoolteachers (in Oron, Moselle) or priests (in Lagarde and Morhange/Riche, Moselle), who might or might not be members of Le Souvenir français (a French association founded in 1887, which maintained war memorials and kept alive the collective memory).

These were the very first German–French 'joint' cemeteries created in August 1914 (Lagarde, Riche, Chicourt, Le Donon),[26] the first French cemeteries (Cutting, Wisches, Vergaville),[27] mass graves (Frémery, Bréhain)[28] or mass French–German graves (Dieuze). Cemeteries were landscaped and possessed monumental crosses (Riche), a 'joint' commemorative memorial (Chicourt)[29] or individual stone memorials (Lagarde).[30] With the first clashes in 1914, The Morhange Garrison Cemetery became multinational. Once reconstructed after the war or according to the standardisation policies, the landscapes of these sites lost some of their originality in the late 1930s. Some escaped having to conform, including Guebwiller,[31] La Forestière[32] and Le Sourd[33] National Cemeteries. Combined pressure from the local population and joint authorities allowed retention of the original semicircle and woodland characteristics, even though the German graves encircled the French ones. After the war, Le Souvenir français maintained the decoration of the cemetery with flowers, a privilege it retained along with the National French Cemetery of La Forestière, where this was also done to honour the wishes of the widow of Captain Jean de Martimprey (missing in action). Born in Brittany, she requested that white, red and blue hydrangeas be planted at each grave and at the cemetery's

Plateau French National Cemetery, Rossignol, Luxembourg, Belgium, 1920–24

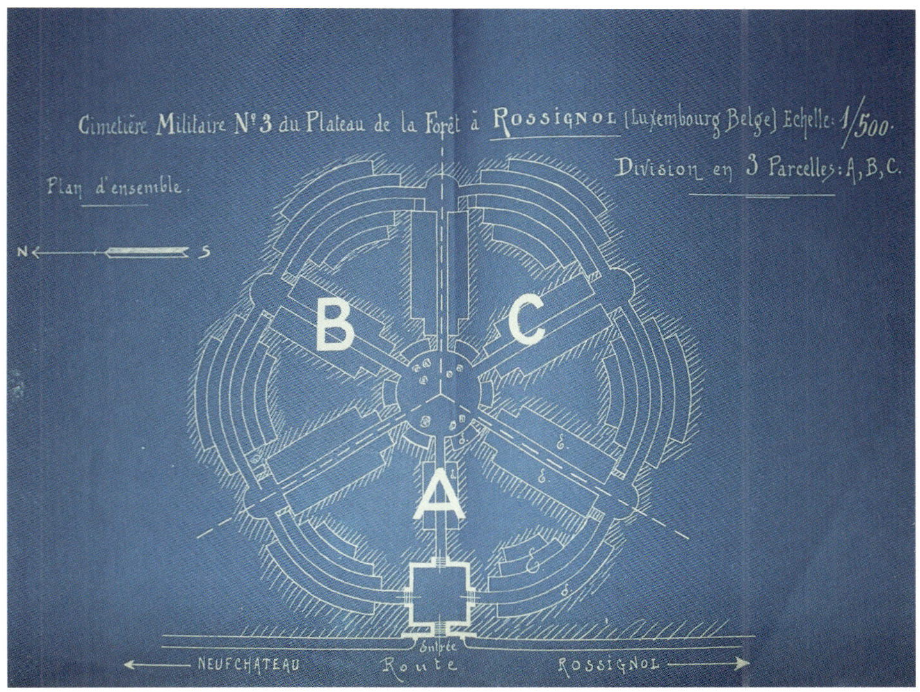


Map of the Plateau French War Cemetery, Rossignol, Luxembourg, Belgium, 1920–24

entrance, in order to mark out the memorial garden in the national colours. The multinational French–German cemetery in Le Sourd kept its layout, Calvary cross, individual headstones (including monumental ones for officers) and centenary rhododendrons.

Both located in Wallonia and designed by Germans, the Plateau French National Cemetery in Rossignol[34] and the Radan French National Cemetery in Bellefontaine perfectly combine the essence of a woodland cemetery with geometrical plans.

Alone or in collaboration with the Army, some priests took the initiative in dealing with the burial of the dead. In 1914, Abbé Alphonse Collé created and landscaped the National Cemetery of Saint-Benoît-la-Chipotte in the Vosges.[35] A year later, he erected the first French memorial of the war, a truncated column in marble honouring the memory of the young soldiers.

In 1915 the Chasseurs Alpins, the elite mountain infantry of the French Army, founded their own cemeteries: Père Duchesne woodland cemetery,[36] Linge[37] and Moosch.[38] They personalised the sites, building chapels in the first two and a Calvary cross in each. Architect Robert Danis (1879–1949) was to use the same symbol at the Hartmannswillerkopf (Vieil Armand), where a chapel was built on the edge of the battlefield, on the axis of the memorial and the cemetery, complying with the state's wish not to include religious associations in its cemeteries.[39]

Priests continued pursuing this task after the war. In April 1919, Paul Doncœur, a Jesuit priest and chaplain of the 28th Brigade, returned to the battlefield of autumn 1915 and was horrified to find the discarded bodies of fallen comrades who had died four years earlier. Enlisting the help of ten volunteers from the 28th Brigade, he moved the decaying remains and gave them graves at the very place where the Brigade's trench lines had been. The magnificent architecture of the granite memorial and cemetery is characterised by a double row of stone crosses and headstones set in a circle, like Celtic standing stones, surrounding an imposing east-facing Calvary cross.[40] Doncoœr was also responsible for the Charles Péguy Memorial at Villeroy (Seine-et-Marne).

Marie-Marguerite Wibrotte continued refurbishing the cemetery in Friscati and erected a memorial there in 1927. Paying tribute to his son Henry and his son's comrades, American citizen William Farnsworth was involved in the monumental design of the Foreign Legion Cemetery in Souain.[41] Inaugurated on 3 November 1920, the monument was designed by the French architect Alexandre Marcel (1860–1928), known for his elaborate projects for the Belgian Crown.

On the Eastern Front, Le Souvenir français diligently worked alongside priests to carry out burials and the first regrouping of bodies. In Grandfontaine (Bas-Rhin), Le Souvenir français had a significant influence on the selection of the location and the architecture of the Le Donon National Cemetery.[42] With its rose-coloured sandstone, the rich geology of the Vosges region gave its headstones and monuments a distinguishing characteristic, but natural stone was gradually replaced by coloured concrete.

While from late 1918 to early 1919 the Commission gave local stakeholders some latitude in dealing with the thousands of burial grounds, their dispersion in the terrain, difficult access and high maintenance costs forced the state to regroup cemeteries.[43] Therefore, the majority of burial grounds disappeared, leaving only those defended by municipalities and families (Pierrepont[44] and Les Éparges[45] National Cemeteries) or supported by figures such as Minister André Maginot (Cutting National Cemetery). There was a shift towards the creation of regrouped sites, copying the model of the Sarrebourg National Cemetery for Prisoners of War (Moselle). The architecture of these graveyards followed the burial regulations of 24 February 1927. The main regrouping cemeteries were La Targette (Battle of Artois), La Crouée (Second

Aerial view of the French National Cemetery at Fleury-devant-Douaumont, Meuse

Battle of the Marne), Rancourt (Battle of the Somme),[46] Craonnelle (Second Battle of the Aisne),[47] but many more were created according to the same plans. The regrouping continued until the 1990s, when the refusal of the local population of Villers-Marmery (Marne) to remove the cemetery seems to have put a halt to the process.[48]

The unique quality of some of the regrouping cemeteries was due to their being created by a combination of ideas that arose via government directives, local community initiatives, associations supported by municipalities and individual action. This was the case for the Saint-Hilaire-le-Grand National Cemetery (Marne),[49] and the Schaeferthal Romanian War Cemetery in Soultzmatt (Haut-Rhin), which remained communal property.[50] In essence, the same holds true for most places of remembrance. **M.-M.D.**

Oriental section, Trabuquet War Cemetery, 1914–19, Menton, Alpes-Maritimes, 2019

1 Archival box 1683, L'Espérance National Cemetery, Cutting (73): correspondence, administrator's deeds, ownership documents, exhumation and reburial records, B 1923, DPMA, Paris.

2 Archival box 1739, Les Entonnoirs (The Funnels), Leintrey, DPMA, Paris.

3 Rémi Dalisson, *Histoire de la mémoire de la Grande Guerre* (Saint-Cloud: Éditions Soteca), 2015.

4 Marie-Thérèse Chabord, 'Le livre d'or de la Première guerre mondiale: un projet sans suite', *Revue historique de l'Armée 2* (1973), pp. 76–89.

5 Gallieni Circular of 17 February 1916, Vincennes, SHD 6V11239.

6 ANBB18/2bis, file 1484A18, Session of 31 May 1919.

7 Antoine Prost, 'Les cimetières militaires et la Grande Guerre, 1914–1940', *Le Mouvement social*, 4/237 (2011), pp. 135–51, available online at <https://www.cairn.info/revue-le-mouvement-social-2011-4-page-135.htm#>.

8 DPMA Archives, Ministry of the Armed Forces, Paris.

9 DPMA Archives, Paris and ONAC/GV Metz.

10 Archival box 1812, Riche National Cemetery (178): correspondence, administrator's deeds, ownership documents, exhumation and reburial records, B 1923, DPMA, Paris.

11 Archival boxes 1843, Sarrebourg National Cemetery, 'War Cemetery for Prisoners of War' (200): correspondence, administrator's deeds, ownership documents, exhumation and reburial records, B 1923, DPMA, Paris.

12 Archival boxes 1756, 1757, 1758, Chambière National Cemetery, Metz (138): ownership documents, administrator's deeds, correspondence, B 1923, DPMA, Paris.

13 Archives, ONAC/GV Metz, Sarrebourg box.

14 Archives, ONAC/GV Metz, Riche box.

15 Remains in the Lagarde Town Hall: stone monuments sculpted during the war.

16 Archival box 1863, La Crouée National Cemetery, Souain-Perthes-lès-Hurlus (215): correspondence, administrator's deeds, ownership documents, exhumation and reburial records, lists of buried soldiers, B, DPMA, Paris.

17 Archival box 1786, La Targette National Cemetery, Neuville-Saint-Vaast (154): ownership documents, administrator's deeds, correspondence, B, DPMA, Paris.

18 Archival boxes 1707, 1708, 1709, Douaumont National Cemetery, Fleury-devant-Douaumont (95): correspondence, administrator's deeds (Ossuary Committee), ownership documents, B, 1924, DPMA, Paris.

19 Archival boxes 1898,1699-1705, Notre-Dame-de-Lorette National Cemetery, Ablain-Saint-Nazaire (1): correspondence, ownership documents, administrator's deeds, B, 1920/2007, DPMA, Paris.

20 Meuse-Argonne Cemetery, in Dean W. Holt, *American Military Cemeteries* (Jefferson, NC: McFarland & Company), 2010 (2nd edn).

21 Box 2044, Joint committee France/Commonwealth. Organisation: history, presentation, texts, preparatory documents, DPMA, Paris.

22 Gavin Stamp, *The Memorial to the Missing of the Somme* (London: Profile Books), 2006; Jeroen Geurst, *Cemeteries of the Great War by Sir Edwin Lutyens* (Rotterdam: 010 Publishers), 2010.

23 Archival box 1915, Friscati, Lunéville National Cemetery, Vitrimont (256): correspondence, administrator's deeds, ownership documents, exhumation and reburial records, B 1922, DPMA, Paris.

24 Archival box 1663, La Grande Tombe de Villeroy National Cemetery, Chauconin-Neufmontiers (55): correspondence, administrator's deeds, ownership documents, lists of buried soldiers, B, 1923, DPMA, Paris.

25 Archival box 1865, L'Opéra National Cemetery, Souain-Perthes-lès-Hurlus (217). Correspondence, administrator's deeds, ownership documents, B, 1918/2002, DPMA, Paris.

26 Archival boxes 1914/ 2013, ONAC/GV Metz.

27 Archival boxes 1914/ 2014, ONAC/GV Metz.

28 Archival boxes ONAC/GV Metz.

29 Archival boxes Chicourt, ONAC/GV Metz.

30 Visible in the Lagarde Town Hall.

31 Archival box 1724, Waldmatt National Cemetery, Guebwiller (107): correspondence, administrator's deeds, ownership documents, B, 1921, DPMA, Paris.

32 Archival box 1734, La Forestière National Cemetery, Lachalade (116): correspondence, administrator's deeds, ownership documents, exhumation and reburial records, B, DPMA, Paris.

33 Archival box 1740, Le Sourd National Cemetery, Lemé, B, 1950, DPMA, Paris.

34 Archival box 1280, French military cemeteries in Belgium (Rossignol 'Plateau' communal plot): ownership documents, correspondence, list of buried soldiers, administrator's deeds, V, DPMA, Paris.

35 Archival box 1817, Saint-Benoît-la-Chipotte National Cemetery (183): correspondence, administrator's deeds, ownership documents, B, 1935, DPMA, Paris.

36 Archival box 1792, Carrefour Duchesne National Cemetery, Orbey (160): ownership documents, correspondence, administrator's deeds, B, 1927, DPMA, Paris.

37 Archival box, 1791, L'Espérance National Cemetery, Orbey (159): correspondence, administrator's deeds, ownership documents, exhumation and reburial records, B 1938, DPMA, Paris.

38 Archival box 1772, Moosch National Cemetery (146): correspondence, administrator's deeds, ownership documents, B, 1922, DPMA, Paris.

39 Archival box 1918, Le Vieil Armand National Cemetery, Wattwiler, B, 1950, DPMA, Paris.

40 Archival box 1866, 'Cimetière de la 28e Brigade, la ferme des Wacques' National Cemetery, Souain-Perthes-lès-Hurlus (218): correspondence, administrator's deeds, ownership documents, B, 1921, DPMA, Paris.

41 Archival box 1864, 'Foreign Legion Cemetery, American Memorial, Farnsworth Monument' National Cemetery, Souain-Perthes-lès-Hurlus (216): correspondence, administrator's deeds, ownership documents, B, 1921, DPMA, Paris.

42 Archival box 1722, Le Donon National Cemetery, Grandfontaine (105): correspondence, administrator's deeds, ownership documents, exhumation and reburial records, B 1923, DPMA, Paris.

43 The French state also encouraged the Allies to regroup graves, except for cemeteries opened during the war by the Germans (German War Cemetery, Lagarde; German War Cemetery, Pierrepont; joint occupied zone cemetery, Assevent, Cambrai, Solesme).

44 Archival box 1795, Pierrepont National Cemetery (163): ownership documents, correspondence, administrator's deeds, B, 1923, DPMA, Paris.

45 Archival box 1918, Les Éparges National Cemetery, Le Trottcir, B, 1950, DPMA, Paris.

46 Archival box 1801, Rancourt National Cemetery (168): correspondence, administrator's deeds, ownership documents, exhumation and reburial records, B 1934, DPMA, Paris.

47 Archival box 1679, Craonnelle National Cemetery (69): correspondence, administrator's deeds, ownership documents, exhumation and reburial records, B 1957, DPMA, Paris.

48 Archival box 1904, Villers-Marmery National Cemetery, V, 1920/2002, DPMA, Paris.

49 Archival box 1961, Russian necropolis, Saint-Hilaire-le-Grand (Marne): ownership documents, conventions, correspondence, administrator's deeds, lists of buried soldiers, B, 1924/2019, DPMA, Paris.

50 Archival box 1962, National Cemetery, Soultzmatt (Haut-Rhin) (163): ownership documents, correspondence, administrator's deeds, B, 1918/1988, DPMA, Paris.

## Landscapes created by the American Battle Monuments Commission

After the First World War, the question as to whether or not to leave the American fallen where they had died raised internal debates in the United States, along with genuine diplomatic negotiations, particularly with France and Belgium.[1] Although the repatriation of bodies was authorised by the United States – contrary to the British government's decision for soldiers of its own empire – many families chose to bury their relatives in European cemeteries.[2]

In 1923, faced with the risk of seeing a multitude of private initiatives, the state administration decided to set up the American Battle Monuments Commission (ABMC), in charge of defining the design and construction of American monuments abroad, along with their maintenance and management.[3] According to its then chairman, General John J. Pershing, the role of the Commission consisted in affirming in the landscape the 'decisive' role of the 'bloody sacrifice' of US servicemen and servicewomen in the victory of the Allies.[4]

Two architects were to successively lead the projects, from the creation of the Commission until the end of the works following the Second World War: Paul Cret, a French-born American architect and designer known for his pure neoclassic style; after Cret's death in 1947, his associate, John F. Harbeson.[5]

The designs of the First World War cemetery landscapes all worked towards the same single objective: the idealisation of the American collective effort. All aspects conformed with this: a spacious chequerboard plan punctuated with conifers, the axis centred on the American flag, a series of narrow paths to access the groups of graves, uniform headstones each with their own generous space, the minimal carving on the headstones ... In this context, individual expression was shunned, particularly regarding differences in rank and even in skin colour – an innovation made easier by the fact that the cemeteries were situated on European soil.

The only differences that were indicated were the religious faith of each dead, the resting place of each body being marked by a concrete Christian cross or a Star of David. The very simple classical style of the monuments and architectural details, and a search for a 'Greek simplicity', contributed to this one single projection of abstraction and European kinship.[6] However, the choice of a neo-Gothic architectural style for the design of chapels perpetuated the tradition found in American civilian cemeteries, which proved to be a reassuring concession to the official authorities and the families alike (similar to the allowances made by those who created the nondenominational cemeteries in America in the nineteenth century). The medieval references made in some decoration contributed in affirming a shared culture with Europe and the interpretation of the American intervention as participation in a Crusade.[7]

Map of the Oise-Aisne American Cemetery, Seringes-et-Nesles, Aisne, WW1

Map of the Lorraine American Cemetery, Saint-Avold, Moselle, WW2

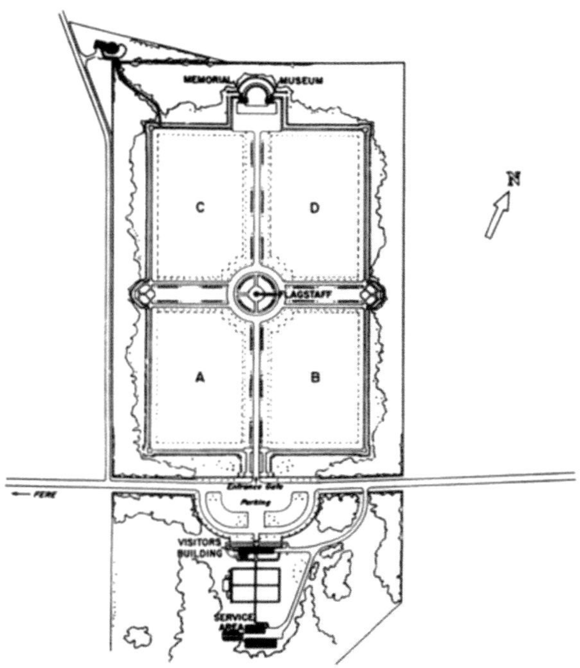


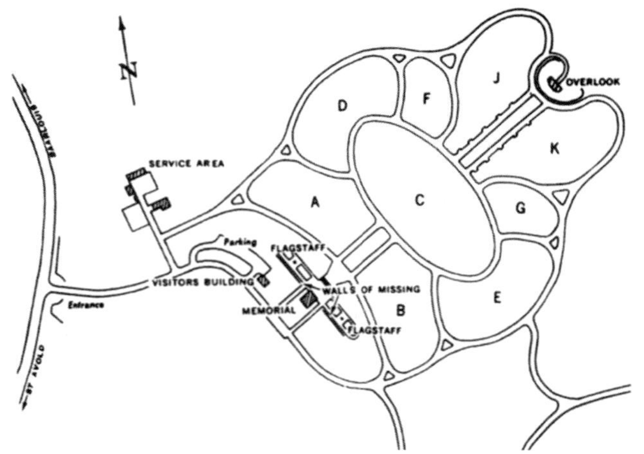


Like the American cemeteries of the First World War, those of the Second World War were located near battlefields, but they offered a very different landscape to that of the 1920s military burial grounds. Far from the grids of graves interspersed with sombre conifers, these monuments incorporated abundant and colourful flower decoration, and boasted curved and asymmetric shapes characteristic of the post-war modernist landscaping that idealised progress and the future. As visitors enter through the chapel, they are presented with an official interpretation of the role of the American troops during the war, before they walk out into a landscape marked by a small number of massive monuments laden with simple symbols, such as the Bald Eagle evoking the protective power of the United States.

At dusk, in some cemeteries, a soundscape accompanies the visual impact, with the playing of the 'The Star-Spangled Banner' followed immediately by the lowering and folding of the flag to the sound of 'Taps', the US Army's bugle call. The American Second World War cemetery landscape as a complete experience is testimony of the image projected by the United States and its huge effort to broadcast it during the post-war years. **M.R.**

1 See the remarkable article by Ron Robin, from which we drew our inspiration: Ron Robin, 'Diplomatie et commémoration: les cimetières américains en France (1918–1955)', *Revue d'Histoire moderne et contemporaine* 42/1 (1995), pp. 126–41.

2 Even after the Second World War, a third of corpses remained in Europe.

3 The ABMC manages and maintains 24 cemeteries and 25 war memorials and other remembrance places.

4 General John J. Pershing was former Commander in Chief of the US troops in Europe during the First World War.

5 Paul Cret himself designed the Château-Thierry American Monument (Aisne), as well as a memorial in Varennes-en-Argonne (Meuse).

6 See, for example, the Château-Thierry American Monument designed by Paul Cret: Robin, op. cit., pp. 131 and 133 (fig. 1).

7 Ibid., p. 131.

## Memorial avenues, or when landscape became memorial

When the First World War broke out, the landscape of Europe was dominated by tree-lined avenues, a landscaping element that dated back to the fifteenth century and that became gradually more evident during the nineteenth century. The number of trees lining French main roads tripled between 1825 and 1895, reaching almost three million specimens, while the Belgian's royal avenues boasted 800,000 on a territory twenty times smaller. It was in this landscape of omnipresent trees that soldiers converged towards the front. For the British and American soldiers marching along these avenues, the military rigour of these long tree-lined roads that flanked their march and channelled their energy towards the battlefield had a taste of the exotic. As the men steadily approached the front line, the avenue became a path bordered with dark, skeletal and shredded trees. British landscape artist Paul Nash (1889–1946) and French writer Henri Barbusse (1873–1935) saw here an analogy with the broken limbs of their brothers in arms. The avenue had become only a trace, and the ghosts of the trees soon disappeared too. When, miracle of miracles, avenues survived in desolate fields, they shone like beacons of hope, like the ultimate vestiges of civilisation before disorder and destruction. They were the memory of order. Tree-lined avenues became a motif that filled letters and stories, paintings and photographs.

In his book *Letters from Flanders*, written in 1915 and published in England the following year, British officer Alexander D. Gillespie writes, 'I had suggested casually that when the peace comes they might make a great road, all along the line of this western front, with a broad strip of ground on either side well planted with fruit trees and trees for shade. It would be a useful war memorial, for a great road is always useful. It might be made most beautiful too …'[1]

Fascinated by botany and a lover of the earth, Gillespie also referred in his book to the Arlington National Cemetery near to Washington, DC. He remembered it as 'a beautiful garden', a park that is 'not in the least a morbid place like most cemeteries'.[2] The avenue which he would have dreamed of would not be a Via Dolorosa but, rather, a Via Sacra – a sacred path where every man, woman and child could learn 'about war […] from the silent witnesses planted on each side of the path'.

In spring 1915, in the Antipodes, far away from the European Continent, Australian citizens were starting to plant avenues. Each planted tree had a name plate fixed to it in tribute to one of their own who had gone to war. Contributed by those who had stayed behind, these avenues created a link with those who were absent and a built a psychological defence against uncertainty and the fear of the ultimate sacrifice. These avenues drew dispersed, suffering communities closer together and at the same time gave the missing the promise of an 'anchor' in their homeland, an image frequently used by the Army's recruitment services.

It was not long before the fallen had to be honoured. The issues of bereavement and suitable locations to mourn the dead became acutely current, particularly for families in distant parts of the British Empire and those in the United States, due to the remoteness of the burial grounds – a problem that was even more crucial in the absence of a grave, since half the fallen of the First World War had disappeared without trace. What kind of war memorial would prove the most effective and glorious for a community wanting to heal itself, albeit without forgetting, once peace had returned? To pay tribute to war heroes, trees like living beings that linked the earth to the heavens were deemed more suitable than 'marble, with its cadaverous whiteness'. Moreover, the longevity of trees was an eternal promise to remember the events in which they had taken part. Braving storms, trees also symbolised courage, while their vigour evoked that of young recruits. Moreover, each spring, the rebirth of nature would seem to be evidence of the victory of life over death. Avenues honouring

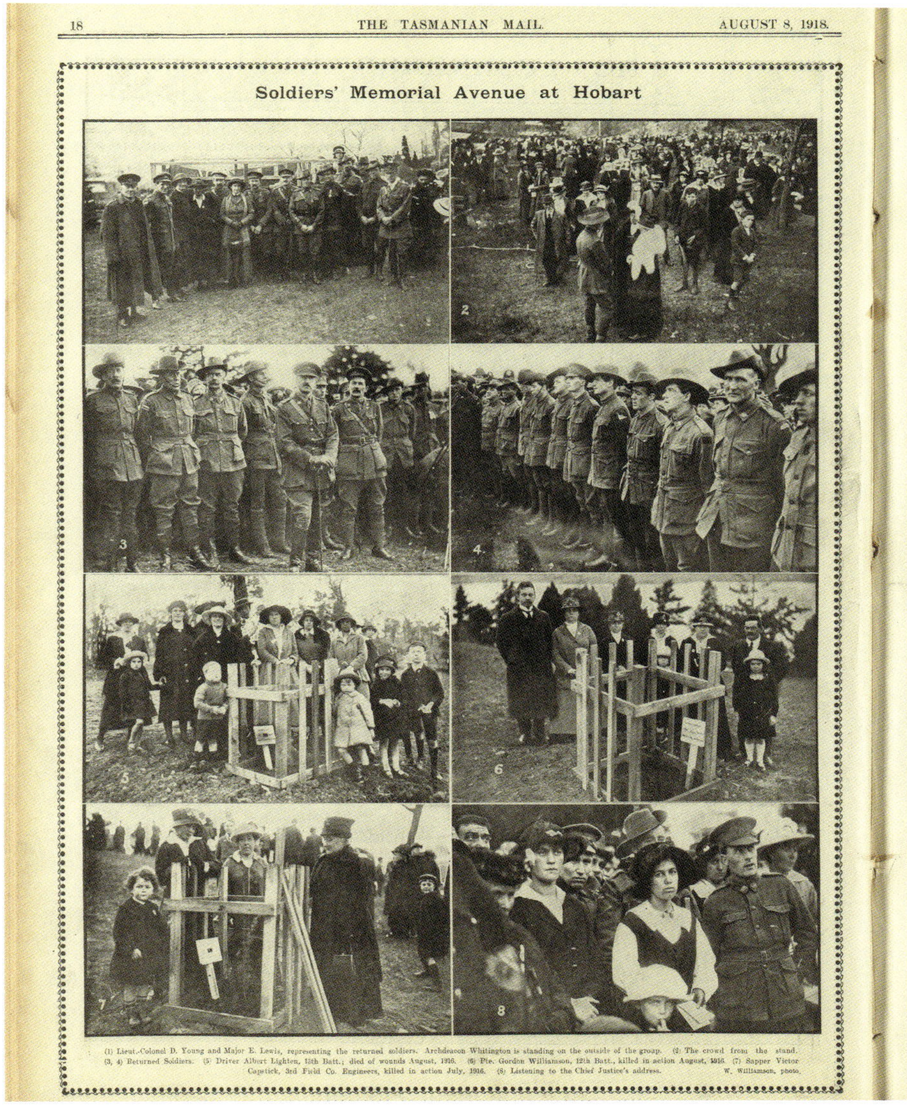

18 THE TASMANIAN MAIL. AUGUST 8, 1918.

Soldiers' Memorial Avenue at Hobart

(1) Lieut.-Colonel D. Young and Major E. Lewis, representing the returned soldiers. Archdeacon Whitington is standing on the outside of the group. (2) The crowd from the stand. (3, 4) Returned Soldiers. (5) Driver Albert Lighten, 15th Batt.; died of wounds August, 1916. (6) Pte. Gordon Williamson, 12th Batt., killed in action August, 1916. (7) Sapper Victor Capstick, 3rd Field Co. Engineers, killed in action July, 1916. (8) Listening to the Chief Justice's address. W. Williamson, photo.

Soldiers Memorial Avenue, Hobart, Australia, in *The Tasmanian Mail*, 8 August 1918

Avenue of Honour, Woodend, Victoria, Australia, WW1

Name plate for the tree planted by the parents of Australian Lieutenant William T. Walsh, WW1

those going to the front – and especially those who never returned – were planted in Australia, Canada, New Zealand, the United States, England and Italy. When assigned to the bereaved family, the action of planting to some extent replaced the interment. Even more so when – as was mostly the case – each tree came with a name plate or small headstone bearing the name of the victim – the minimum of gestures that could be made in such circumstances.

Lined up along a route, a road or a path, these trees also recalled columns of soldiers. In these homogeneous whole entities, each tree – like each solider – has its own personality. In effect, the soldiers identified with the trees in a very powerful way, which some witnesses of the time recalled as giving rise to very moving gestures.

These avenues of remembrance, which could be seen as private memorials inseparable from the public space – which some compared to the Roman Via Appia (Appian Way), originally constructed as a military road – preserve the memory of the sacrifice of these men and women more effectively than a common monument. These places of significant importance were carefully chosen and the scope was often extremely ambitious, such as the 1918 plan to plant the 5,454-kilometre Lincoln Highway linking New York and San Francisco, or a proposal in New Zealand in 1936 to plant the 640-kilometre road from Auckland to Wellington, making it a great Memorial Highway. In fact, although impressive, the avenues that were realised were more modest: 40 kilometres in York County for the Lincoln Highway; 50 kilometres for New Zealand's Memorial Highway; while, in Australia, the Ballarat Avenue of Honour and its 3,800 trees ran the length of 23 kilometres and the Calgary Memorial Drive in Canada with its 3,278 trees achieved 9.5 kilometres.

These memorial projects also recalled the avenues in Europe, which had ordered the countryside, cities and gardens for centuries. The long French roads that had been paced by the soldiers were explicitly evoked during various inaugurations: they were cited by the Minister for Recruitment in Concord, Australia, in June 1918, and by his counterpart in Des Moines, United States, in 1922. The press also made this connection, evoking Louisiana's Jefferson Highway in 1921 and New Zealand's Wanganui Memorial Avenue in 1938. In 1919, US senator and future president Warren Harding felt that planting trees to honour American soldiers was a 'useful and beautiful idea' that the soldiers 'had brought back from France'. The option of using poplar trees reinforced the relationship – presumed or claimed – with French roads.

Beyond the 'more natural' countryside avenues, in 1921, on the occasion of the planting of the first *Platanus* bordering the avenue of remembrance in Victoria, Canada, reference was made to 'pleasure boulevards', such as London's Mall or Paris's Champs-Élysées. At the inauguration of Minneapolis's Victory Memorial Drive – 568 trees planted for soldiers and nurses – the allusion was to the kind of avenues found in parks and gardens. Memorial avenues were designed to provide beautification of the whole environment for everybody, much in the same way as trees planted in lines during the nineteenth century in newly conquered lands appeared like instruments of civilisation. In 1913, referring to European tree-lined avenues, the US Bureau of Education invited schools to plant trees along roads, edging the Good Roads Movement closer to what became known as Arbor Day. The attitudes of the American, Australian and New Zealand press were not far behind – before, during and after the war, they extolled the omnipresence of trees along French roads and streets, and encouraged their citizens to draw inspiration from the magnificent French example. It is thus hardly surprising that Ballarat – in 1859 one of the first cities in Australia to decorate its streets with lines of trees – should also have planted the longest driveway in the country. Nor is it unexpected that the Oamaru Beautifying Society, with its planting of 400 oaks in 1918, should initiate the first Memorial Avenue in New Zealand. Or that, in the United States, with the growth of the automobile sector, memorial avenues were also parkways, such as in Cleveland (1918) or Minneapolis (1921). Or that the Roads of Remembrance Association, a proponent for memorial planting in England, combined with the Roads Beautifying Association founded in 1928. **C.P.**

---

1 2nd Lieut. A. D. Gillespie, *Letters from Flanders* (London: Smith, Elder & Co.), 1916, p. 232; available online at <https://archive.org/details/lettersfromfland00gilluoft/page/n7>.

2 Ibid., p. 234.

## Topographies of remembrance across the former British Empire

Where once geographers could argue that the ideological and aesthetic issues surrounding the military cemeteries created by the British Empire had drawn little comment, there is now a considerable literature exploring the spaces and places of remembrance. Increasing attention has been paid during the past decade to the value of 'situation' in the discourse of death, grieving and commemoration. In this respect, 'situation' should be understood to be a focus on 'place', 'space' and the geopolitical.[1] The emerging discipline of cultural geography in the late 1990s created the tools necessary to elaborate 'space' in the abstract, to regard 'place' as a site where an individual might negotiate definitively social relations, and give voice, as Sara Blair argued, to 'the effects of dislocation, disembodiment, and localisation that constitute contemporary social disorder'.[2] Almost a century after Sigmund Freud's treatise *Mourning and Melancholia*, our understanding of how memory and mourning function continues to be challenged, revised and refined. Issues of place have become important to this debate. Once a marginal topic for academic investigation, there is now a body of scholarly work – including deep research in landscape and garden design – that explores the complex interrelationship between memory, mourning and 'death-scapes' (or 'memory-scapes'), a portmanteau term that fuses an appreciation of once-violated landscapes with personal and discursive memories.[3]

Across the former British Empire during and after the First World War, there was a long and complicated debate about the 'proper' forms of remembrance. There was an intense dispute about the repatriation of bodies and a public argument about the best way to mark the sites of burial. As the protocols of commemoration were debated and agreed, a delicate balance was struck between permanent stone markers and horticultural proxies for memory achieved through the planting of trees, shrubs, flowers and turfed lawn.

In his seminal text on cultural histories, David Lowenthal has argued that landscape is 'memory's most serviceable reminder'.[4] He suggests that certain places can be regarded as key sites in a continuous educational process, where successive generations 'revise or expand their cultural memory through interaction with the artefacts and landscapes of its past.' Former battlefields are critical places in Lowenthal's taxonomy of significance. This is because they are not a single, sealed terrain isolated in a given moment of time; they are multivocal landscapes of accretion stratified by overlapping layers of social, economic and occasionally political history. Invariably, they are also politicised, dynamic, and open to constant negotiation.[5] Official sites of mass burial, ornamented with august memorials and strict planting regimes, have not only long provided 'pegs' upon which national fiction could be hung, but flag posts from which declarations of national identity and purpose can be articulated. Others have argued that the marking of a battlefield with monuments, memorials and markers fulfils a natural human need to understand, possess, classify and control what happened, 'so that it is manageable, even if not wholly explicable'.[6] Explication, however, needs a certain degree of authentication; and achieving authenticity is rarely straightforward. It requires careful manipulation and even contrivance. These issues of 'contrivance', 'manipulation' and 'authenticity' are still hotly debated today: we see this in the Dardanelles peninsula in Turkey where the Australian preferences for national memory are contested by the Turkish, and in South Africa and New Zealand where the marking of indigenous histories arouses passionate debate about the appropriate lens of remembering. The recent centenary of the end of the First World War gave further opportunities for the marking of time and place, including many significant creative events, installations and artistic interventions that adopted a temporal discourse, and left a less permanent marking of the sites of battle.

**Imagination and immutable memory**

In a lecture given at the New York Public Library, and later published as 'The Site of Memory', the author Toni Morrison suggested that so-called 'fictional' writing is rarely a product of complete invention, but is always an act of imagination bound up with memory: 'You know, they straightened out the Mississippi River in places, to make room for houses and livable acreage. Occasionally, the river floods these places. "Floods" is the word they use, but in fact it is not flooding; it is remembering. Remembering where it used to be. All water has a perfect memory and is forever trying to get back to where it was.'[7]

Morrison's poetic image of a 'stream of memory' compelled to revisit an original site can be seen as integral to the relationship between geographical spaces and the construction of individual and collective remembering. This syncretic intertwining of place, identity and memory is rare and subject to a continuous evolution of meaning.[8] Social memory links emotional ties with specific geographies that are anchored in 'places past'. Most often during periods of national commemoration, appropriate emotions have been invested in enduring stone, bronze or brick, their monumental forms strewn across our urban landscape. M. Christine Boyer has described such manifestations as 'rhetorical topoi ... civic compositions that teach us about our national heritage and our public responsibilities and assume that the urban landscape itself is the emblematic embodiment of power and memory'.[9] In Wellington, New Zealand, not content with the impressive War Memorial building and Carillon tower, the authorities have created a large commemorative precinct that reinstates the garden design and axial layout of the memorial roadways. Tunnels to divert traffic have been dug, trees repositioned, appropriate shrubs planted. Perhaps the *pièce de résistance* is the restrained tomb-like sculpture created by Kingsley Baird, located with greatly subtlety on the steps of the monument, which acts as the repository for the remains of an Unknown Warrior returned from Flanders in 2004.

The meaning of traditional monuments is problematic. Lewis Mumford asserted that revered sites rapidly become invisible within the collective memory because 'something has impregnated them against attention'.[10] They simply blend back into the undifferentiated landscape. In short, the meaning of monuments, like memory itself, is profoundly unstable.[11] It is thus hardly surprising that, after each of the world wars of the last century, the dialectic between remembering and forgetting has been a dominant theme in the discourses around commemoration and remembrance.[12] Analysing what he refers to as the 'anxiety of erasure' engendered by bourgeois culture, Thomas Laqueur asserts that figurative simulation – the plinth-bound statue – has long been inadequate to the task entrusted to it. Instead, 'the thing itself must do because representation can no longer be relied on',[13] as those who understand the power of nature, of site and the poetics of place recognise that 'the thing' may often be little more than a cleared and uncluttered tract of land to which historic significance is attached.

A semiotics of place has been clearly articulated by the French sociologist Maurice Halbwachs, who was compelled by the qualities of particular sites and examined their role in the formation of collective memory. 'Space', wrote Halbwachs, 'is a reality that endures', it can unite groups of individuals and believers concentrating and 'moulding its character to theirs'.[14] When compared to transient phenomena

Beaumont-Hamel Newfoundland Memorial, Somme, WW1. Aerial view showing the Caribou statue and the front-line trenches, 2012

and ill-considered monumentalia, certain geographical locations appear to offer a sense of legitimate permanence that draws pilgrims to sites that 'place' or 'contain' the memory of overwhelming events. The terrain around the Brandenburg Gate, surrounding Les Invalides, the 'grassy knoll' in downtown Dallas, might be considered secular shrines that are capable of rekindling memories of awesome events. Claudia Koonz, in an analysis of the commemorative hinterland around Nazi concentration camps, suggests that whereas we know that written texts are 'infinitely malleable' and readily abridged, films edited and photographs airbrushed, the landscape feels immutable. Only geography, she argues, is capable of conveying the narrative of extermination: 'At these places of remembering, memory feels monolithic, unambiguous, and terrible.'[15] It is a point endorsed by James Mayo, in his epic survey of the contested terrain of native North America, when he simply states: 'the landscape itself is the memorial'.[16]

However, such a fundamental understanding of the power of place has not deterred those who wish to further furnish the memorial landscape. Across northern France and Belgium, the countryside has become liberally littered with plaques, texts and markers, as the former Empire and Dominion countries seek to inscribe their versions of the past. The process of re-marking the land appears unquenchable and at times factionalised. The stone obelisk funded by the Loyal Orange Institution of Northern Ireland and situated at the site of a notorious German machine-gun post called 'The Pope's Nose' on the Somme was for a period after its erection in 1993 regularly damaged by opposition groups who allegedly contested its sectarian authority. Not far distant, 60 years after the original memorial financed by public subscription was unveiled in 1926, the South African government further expanded their existing memorial on the Somme site, adding a building in the form of a five-pointed star to convey their narrative of the war. The potency of the site is deepened by its arboreal surroundings. Delville Wood, 63 hectares of preserved terrain, is still pitted with shell craters and old trench lines; a much-scarred hornbeam is held to be 'The Last Tree' to have survived the war, and a double avenue of oaks was grown from acorns gathered from original trees that French Huguenot Jean Gardiol had brought to South Africa in 1688. More recently, in 2002, a beech tree has been planted in remembrance of two soldiers from the Royal Welch Fusiliers who died in July 1916.

Such sites of memory, or '*lieux de mémoire*' as understood by Pierre Nora, exist at the intersection between official (or civic) and vernacular cultures.[17] Their inestimable value to the workings of collective memory is recognised by John Gillis, who points out that 'most people find it difficult to remember without having access to mementos, images, and physical sites to objectify their memory'.[18] Preservation and 'reconstruction' of such sites has accelerated recently, alongside a compulsive consumption of personal and public history, and the democratisation (some might say privatisation) of the past. At the South African site in Delville Wood, there is clearly a dialogue between state-sanctioned build (in stone and glass) and populist intervention (through planting and preservation of natural motifs). A similar dialogue between public and personal has been created at the National Memorial Arboretum in Staffordshire, central England, which combines the rhetorical topography of nationhood in stone, bronze and cast metal, alongside private messages of remembering appended as texts and labels to trees, shrubs and copses.

## 'Memory-scapes'

Few sites and occasions can hold such grave esteem in the recent history of the British Empire than the dawn service held at Anzac Cove in Gallipoli on 25 April. Every year thousands of young Australians and New Zealanders make the long pilgrimage to the killing grounds defended by the Turkish and German armies in 1915.

Perched on the tip of the Dardanelles peninsula in western Turkey, these tiny battlefields offer a telling example of a heritage site that has been spasmodically contested by 'insiders and outsiders' since British Empire troops evacuated its bloody ridges and exposed beaches in January 1916. The defence of Gallipoli was a victory for the Turkish army – their single triumph in five campaigns – but until very recently this might not be the first impression gained by any visitor. The peninsula is peppered with British and Allied war memorials, battlefield museums, facsimile trench lines and military cemeteries. The main period of cemetery planning and memorial building took place in the 1920s, carved in the restrained neoclassical style that characterises the work of the Imperial War Graves Commission under its principal architect, Sir John Burnet.[19]

As for marking their part in the campaign, there was no comparable response from the Turkish authorities until the 1950s and late 1960s when a number of modernist structures were built at Cape Helles, the most southern point of the peninsula. During the late 1980s several traditional Islamic memorial sites were built, and in recent years some large figurative statues – some of them strident, even bombastic, in tenor – have been erected at Anzac and Helles. Although the war ended here in 1916, a battle for monumental supremacy has been waged ever since. Turkish and Commonwealth memorial sites are located uncomfortably close to each other on the cliffs over the once disputed beaches, and immense statues of Turkish heroes stand face to face with Commonwealth War Graves Commission obelisks, locked in 'parallel monologues'.[20] On the eve of the 80th anniversary of the Allied landings in 1995, the Turkish authorities supplemented the martial statuary with an ambitious – but not uncontroversial – planting scheme designed to dress the battlefield with appropriate symbolic floral designs.[21]

Two years later, the Turkish government announced a competition for a new 330,000-hectare park dedicated to peace at Gallipoli. Although a winning design

was chosen, there has been little (indeed, no apparent) progress in advancing the scheme and the only physical changes on the peninsula have been the unplanned encroachment of villas, infrastructure and an irreversible road-widening programme intended to facilitate the tens of thousands of tourists who visit. In recent years, Australian and New Zealand visitors have become concerned at the unsightly violation of a place they deem to be essential to their origins and identity as a modern nation. Their objection and resistance appear to be having no impact. Instead, the Turkish state has started to reassert its authority and the 'moral' ownership of the former battleground has shifted palpably.

### Beyond space: creative interventions in recent years

Perhaps the most distinctive aspect of the commemorative period 2014–18 was the contribution of artists, designers and curators in bringing site-specific and time-based work to the sites of military memory. Achieved through both public and private funding, through crowdfunding and fellowships, a diverse population of painters, sculptors, media practitioners and printmakers from across the former British Empire have created some of the most striking icons of commemoration. The art installation *Blood Swept Lands and Seas of Red* at the Tower of London required some 890,000 ceramic poppies to be sculpted, fired and installed by artists and public volunteers.[22] In October 2014, over the Channel in Belgium, 8,750 torchbearers lined the old front line from Nieuwpoort to Ploegsteert as it existed in November 1914.[23] A few years later, sculptor Koen Vanmechelen placed 600,000 individually fired clay sculptures along a tract of the old front line a few miles from Ypres, at a notorious section known as '*Die Grosse Bastion*', also known as 'The Bluff'.[24]

The very transience of these art events seemed to add to their popular appeal. They became a distinctive feature of the memorial landscape. Because most were time-based and site-specific there was a strong overlap with film and theatre – most notably in the work of New Zealand film director Peter Jackson, whose extraordinary exhibition *Gallipoli: The Scale of Our War* and installations of oversize models of soldiers and nurses at the Museum of New Zealand Te Papa Tongarewa, Wellington, attracted global media attention. In scale and reach his work is redolent of the panoramas and theatrical spectacles that attracted huge crowds, and many soldiers on leave, during the Great War itself. Another Oscar-winning film director, Danny Boyle, choreographed a nationwide commemorative event on beaches across Britain. The public were asked to join together to create huge silhouettes in the sand of people who died in the war. Images were available from the national 'Lives of the First World War' project, which aimed to tell the stories of eight million people from across the British Empire who served. Such nationwide temporal events proved hugely popular with people of all backgrounds, gaining extensive news coverage and reaching out in ways that more conventional displays of an historical past – battlefield tours, unveiling of memorials, re-enactment events – could not do.

Commemoration offered opportunities not only to remember and revisit artwork from the period, but to create highly memorable and moving works of new art. Turner prizewinner Jeremy Deller devised a human memorial, *We're Here Because We're Here*, by sending out 1,500 silent soldiers across British cities and towns during a single day: 1 July 2016, the 100th anniversary of the Battle of the Somme. South African artist and polymath William Kentridge created the epic *The Head & the Load* in 2018 to tell the neglected story of the millions of African porters and carriers who served British, French and German forces during the war.[25] In Australia, the Federal Government commissioned two Victorian artists who had served as Australian Official War Artists in Afghanistan and Iraq. Charles Green and Lyndell Brown designed a large tapestry for the Sir John Monash Centre on the Somme. *Morning Star* depicts a winter dawn light illuminating a path through the Australian eucalyptus bush. The composition is inset with portraits of soldiers and fragments showing embarkation and arrival. Like so many remarkable artworks commissioned during the commemorative period, the artists wanted to stress both the historical aspect and its resonance in the present: 'The tapestry emphasises the disjunction between the terrible experiences that the museum describes rather than repeats them. It seems to us very important to present images such as soldiers might have carried in their hearts and imaginations as they arrived at the Western Front.'[26] **P.G.**

---

This text draws on some previously published material: namely, Paul Gough, 'Sites in the Imagination: The Beaumont Hamel Newfoundland Memorial on the Somme', *Cultural Geographies* 11/3 (2004), pp. 235–58.

1 John R. Gillis (ed.), *Commemorations: The Politics of National Identity* (Princeton, NJ: Princeton University Press), 1994; George L. Mosse, *Fallen Soldiers: Reshaping the Memory of the World Wars* (New York: Oxford University Press), 1990; Mandy S. Morris, 'Gardens "For Ever England": Landscape, Identity and the First World War British Cemeteries on the Western Front', *Ecumene* 4/4 (1997), pp. 410–34; George McKay, *Radical Gardening: Politics, Idealism and Rebellion in the Garden* (London: Frances Lincoln), 2011.

2 Sara Blair, 'Cultural Geography and the Place of the Literary', *American Literary History* 10/3 (1998), pp. 544–67, here p. 544.

3 Paul Basu, 'Palimpsest Memoryscapes: Materializing and Mediating War and Peace in Sierra Leone', in Ferdinand de Jong and Michael Rowlands (eds), *Reclaiming Heritage: Alternative Imaginaries of Memory in West Africa* (Walnut Creek, CA: Left Coast Press), 2007, pp. 231–59.

4 David Lowenthal, *The Past is a Foreign Country* (Cambridge: Cambridge University Press), 1985, p. 11.

5 Barbara Bender (ed.), *Landscape: Politics and Perspectives* (Oxford: Berg), 1993. See also Barbara Bender and Margot Winer (eds), *Contested Landscapes: Movement, Exile and Place* (Oxford: Berg), 2001.

6 Jennifer Iles, 'Recalling the Ghosts of War: Performing Tourism on the Battlefields of the Western Front', *Text and Performance Quarterly* 26/2 (2006), pp. 162–80.

7 Toni Morrison, 'The Site of Memory', in Russell Ferguson, Martha Gever, Trinh T. Minh-ha and Cornel West (eds), *Out There: Marginalization and Contemporary Cultures* (New York/Cambridge, MA: The New Museum of Contemporary Art/The MIT Press), 1990, pp. 299–326, here p. 305.

National Memorial Arboretum, Alrewas, Staffordshire, inaugurated in 2001, 2018

Ari Burnu Memorial inscribed with words attributed to Turkey's founding father, Mustafa Kemal Atatürk, Ari Burnu Cemetery, Çanakkale battlefield site, Gallipoli historic district, Turkey, 2017

8 For an elaboration of syncretism, see Nuala C. Johnson, 'Mapping monuments: the shaping of public space and cultural identities', *Visual Communication* 1/3 (2002), pp. 293–98, here p. 294.

9 M. Christine Boyer, *The City of Collective Memory: Its Historical Imagery and Architectural Entertainments* (Cambridge, MA: The MIT Press), 1996, p. 321. See also Jeremy Foster, 'Creating a tenemos, positing "South Africanism": material memory, landscape practice, and the circulation of identity at Delville Wood', *Cultural Geographies* 11/3 (2004), pp. 259–90.

10 Lewis Mumford, *The Culture of Cities* (New York: Harcourt, Brace and Co.), 1938, p. 435.

11 Robert Musil, in Marina Warner, *Monument & Maidens: The Allegory of the Female Form* (London: Weidenfeld and Nicholson), 1985, p. 21. See also Daniel J. Sherman, 'Art, Commerce, and the Production of Memory in France after World War I', in John R. Gillis (ed.), *Commemorations: The Politics of National Identity* (Princeton, NJ: Princeton University Press), 1994, pp. 186–211.

12 See Adrian Forty and Susanne Kuchler (eds), *The Art of Forgetting* (Oxford: Berg), 1994; and Adrian Gregory, *The Silence of Memory, Armistice Day 1919–1946* (Oxford: Berg), 1994.

13 Thomas Laqueur, 'The Past's Past' (book review), *London Review of Books* 18/18 (19 September 1996), pp. 3–7.

14 Maurice Halbwachs, *The Collective Memory*, intro. Mary Douglas, trans. F. J. Ditter Jr and V. Y. Ditter (New York: Harper Colophon), 1980. First published as *La Mémoire collective*, 1950, p. 178.

15 Claudia Koonz, 'Between Memory and Oblivion: Concentration Camps in German Memory', in John R. Gillis (ed.), *Commemorations: The Politics of National Identity* (Princeton, NJ: Princeton University Press), 1994, pp. 258–80, here p. 259.

16 James M. Mayo, *War Memorials as Political Landscape: The American Experience and Beyond* (New York: Praeger), 1988, p. 172.

17 Pierre Nora (ed.), *Realms of Memory: The Construction of the French Past*. Volume 1, *Conflicts and Divisions*; Volume 2, *Traditions*; Volume 3, *Symbols* (New York: Columbia University Press), 1992–6.

18 John R. Gillis, Introduction, 'Memory and Identity: The History of a Relationship', in John R. Gillis (ed.), *Commemorations: The Politics of National Identity* (Princeton, NJ: Princeton University Press), 1994, pp. 3–24, here p. 17.

19 Bruce Scates, *Return to Gallipoli: Walking the Battlefields of the Great War* (Cambridge, Cambridge University Press), 2006.

20 Rosie Ayliffe, Mark Dubin and John Gawthrop, *Turkey: The Rough Guide* (London: Harrap Columbus), 1991, p. 102.

21 Paul Gough, 'Conifers and Commemoration: The Politics and Protocol of Planting in Military Cemeteries', *Landscape Research* 21/1 (1996), pp. 73–87.

22 Designed by Paul Cummins and Tom Piper, the artwork was first created in the moat of the Tower of London, England, between July and November 2014. Further shows of the work toured the UK until 2018, and were staged at St Magnus Cathedral in Orkney, the Black Watch Museum in Perth (Scotland), Ulster Museum in Belfast, Caernarfon Castle in Wales, and other locations.

23 *The Light Front*, 2014, staged on 17 October 2014, from Nieuwpoort to Ploegsteert (south of Ypres), Belgium.

24 Koen Vanmechelen, *ComingWorldRememberMe (CWRM)*, Palingbeek, near Ypres, Belgium, 30 March – 11 November 2018.

25 William Kentridge, *The Head & the Load*, Turbine Hall, Tate Modern, London, 11 to 15 July 2018. The work was co-commissioned by New York's Park Avenue Armory and Duisburg's Ruhrtriennale, with additional support from Holland Festival.

26 From an article about the tapestry in *Woven: Australian Tapestry Workshop* (2017), pp. 5–7. See also, Charles Green and Lyndell Brown, 'No Agency: Iraq and Afghanistan at War – The Perspective of Commissioned War Artists', in Martin Kerby, Margaret Baguley, Janet McDonald (eds), *The Palgrave Handbook of Artistic and Cultural Responses to War since 1914: The British Isles, the United States and Australasia* (Sydney: Palgrave Macmillan), 2019, pp. 23–43.

## War landscapes: their legacy

Cemeteries are the most visible markers in the landscape of the former front line of the First World War. Beyond these evident witnesses, other zones that were devastated are now both cemeteries and more or less landscaped manifestations of remembrance.

Approximately 700,000 bodies of combatants were never recovered and continue to lie in the former battlefields, now an immense necropolis. Every year, on both sides of the Western Front – which ran along 700 kilometres, from the English Channel to the Swiss frontier – corpses of soldiers are unearthed during works carried out in areas claimed back for human activity. In his book *Le paysan des Poilus*, Jean-Luc Pamart resonates with emotion when he tells the story of the land he has cultivated throughout his life in Confrécourt, in the Aisne: 'My wheat, my potatoes, my beets take root in corpses. So, I look at my land differently. You cannot cheat with land.'

To avoid cheating with the landscapes we have inherited from the First World War, we must hold its keys to understanding. While, during the conflict, many soldiers compared the battlefield to the surface of the moon, life has once again taken over, erasing or masking scars that were previously thought to be permanent. Today, many traces are cloaked under a thick coat of trees and the layer of humus that has fallen at their feet. This soil cover proved controversial very early on and for many years.

During the interwar period, while some rejoiced at the rebirth of life on land marked by the wrath of war, others feared that this regeneration would obliterate the memory of the suffering that had been endured. On 4 August 1934 the weekly newspaper *L'Illustration* commented: 'Chaos still exists, but it is veiled. Somehow, plants have regrown. Where men forsake the task, nature went back to work on its own. [...] Today, an ill-informed tourist – if, by any miracle, this type of tourist could exist – could never imagine that a prodigious drama had murdered this earth, eradicating human beings. He would barely be taken aback by the baroque look of the ground's texture.'

### A forest as a bandage

Placed like a bandage on the scars of the land, the Forêt domaniale de Verdun (a national park) is the fruit of this long and difficult debate. The vast forests covering most of the battlefield look nothing like the landscape that overwhelmed the soldiers. They are not even anything like the natural aspect of this area before the conflict took place. In 1914 only 40 per cent of the 150,000 hectares of the quadrilateral zone formed by the forts of Douaumont, Thiaumont, Souville and Vaux were wooded. Around the area's nine villages (now disappeared) were mostly fields, orchards and vineyards, encircled by private and communal woods. Between 21 February and 15 December 1916, some 53 million shells were fired on this zone measuring 5 by 2 kilometres. After the war, most observers were of the opinion that the area could never be repaired. In 1919 the French state classified as 'Red Zones' the territory in which the cost of restoration would be higher than its value in 1914. This ranking was applied to approximately 19,500 hectares in the Meuse and prompted a crucial question: what must be done with these abandoned lands that have a completely unprecedented legal status?

From 1921 onwards, plants began to spontaneously reclaim the battlefield. Grass, moorland, thorny and woody thickets were already blurring the scars on the ground, much to the chagrin of veterans. In 1923 the state expropriated most of the devastated land around Verdun and entrusted it to a forestry administration put in charge of implementing the unusual idea that a forestry worker veteran had come up with: (re)forest the area to transform the Verdun region into an immense sanctuary. Thirty-six million trees planted in just eight years created a new environment that seems to have won the difficult wager of allying the rebirth of the earth and the memories of humankind's suffering.

### Resilience in oblivion or remembrance gardening?

Today the Forêt domaniale de Verdun, classed as a '*Forêt d'Exception®*', is a source of great pride: the National Forestry Office invites tourists to 'wander around the greatest sites of the 1914–18 War while appreciating the beauty and diversity of the fauna and flora'. Unimaginable in the eyes of some immediately after the war, today this metamorphosis is presented as a success.

While the world confronts unprecedented ecological challenges, Boris Cyrulnik's concept of resilience applied to human beings (as elaborated in his *Resilience: How Your Inner Strength Can Set You Free from the Past*, 2011) shows us – with great hope – the capacity of 'resurrection through pain', demonstrated by the ecosystems devastated by human madness. When we examine the issue more deeply we find that in reality this healing process is more complex, and that hidden in the depths of the earth are harmful, corrosive substances. In Verdun and elsewhere on the former battlefield, thousands of tonnes of unexploded ammunition are still disintegrating, discharging toxic substances that poison the earth, the water table and watercourses. This disturbing reality resurfaced in summer 2015, during First World War commemorations, when the milk and grain production of seven farms in the Meuse had to be destroyed due to pollution by toxic ammunition residue. While today the future of some of this land, still held in protection by the state, is uncertain, farmers and local inhabitants have been shocked to discover the forgotten history of the vast operation to deactivate the toxic ammunition that was initiated in the 1920s. This had been carried out on several agricultural sites spread out around the communes of Muzeray, Vaudoncourt, Loison and Spincourt, to the northeast of Verdun: 1,500,000 chemical shells and 300,000 explosive shells were defused out of sight of the general public, who had been deliberately kept away from the workings of this completely unknown type of factory. It eventually disappeared in 1925 under disturbing circumstances, leaving behind a veritable gaping hole of memory.

Although some of these activities had left their mark on the landscape, particularly in the area known as 'Place à Gaz' (Gas Square) in the Spincourt forest, local inhabitants do not appear to have remembered what happened there. Foresters, who regularly passed through the place, retain a form of consciousness of what occurred, notably through its name. At a moment when, also in the Meuse, the burial of nuclear waste that will remain dangerous for thousands of years is under consideration, the pollution linked to the First World War ammunition is one of the first scientifically documented historic cases to offer a framework for thinking about the long-term effects of toxic waste – making it a memory that impacts across time.

Landscapes are born from the encounter between humankind and nature, and serve as the canvas on which the hopes of our society are drawn. The fate for areas polluted by the detritus of war invites us to consider what we want to do with all the other waste we have produced since the First World War, which provoked a huge turning point in the world's industrial development. How do we keep alive the memory of something unwanted? Is it not tempting to give way to oblivion, by letting nature take back its rights? Or would it be preferable to intervene and keep a lasting memory alive through eternally renewed acts of gardening and nurturing? **I.L.**

Fort de Vaux, Verdun, Meuse, 2017

## From memorials to gardens of peace

If we look at the evolution of the memorialisation of war – from the war memorials established during the Boer War and maintained by the Imperial War Grave Commission, right up to contemporary projects – we can see that the landscape of remembrance has shifted towards less monumental architecture and more natural landscaping. The war memorial was replaced by gardens and landscape installations, evoking peace rather than war, which has been an ongoing trend since the creation of the British war cemetery garden. The preservation of the traces of trenches that constitute the Beaumont-Hamel Newfoundland Memorial or the craters surrounding Fort Douaumont speak more of war and peace than colossal monuments could ever do.

Monumental edifices rewarding bravery have been replaced with landscaped remembrance walls and gardens, especially sunken gardens that dramatise the void, powerful art installations, and the participation of inhabitants as self-proclaimed gardeners of memory and peace. Gardens of peace and memory – such as the Sunken Rose Garden of the Irish National War Memorial Gardens in Dublin (first proposed 1919; opened 1940), designed by Sir Edwin Lutyens – started appearing at the end of the First World War. Aided by anguish about nuclear weapons and the powerful upsurge of peace movements, gardens of peace have proliferated after the disasters of the Second World War. Examples are the Hiroshima Peace Memorial Park, designed in 1954 by Kenzo Tange (1913–2005), on the site created by the atomic bomb; the Nagasaki Peace Park, designed in 1955 by Seibo Kitamura (1884–1987); and the Vietnam Veterans Memorial (within Washington's Constitution Gardens), two long walls of polished granite set into a huge lawn embankment, designed in 1982 by Maya Ying Lin (b. 1959). In 2009 a Garden of Peace was established adjacent to the German Second World War cemetery at La Cambe (Normandy): the bordering hills were planted with 1,200 maple trees, each financed by donations from various countries.

If, with the Memorial to the Murdered Jews of Europe (inaugurated 2005), American architect Peter Eisenman (b. 1932) plays with the whole space – the memorial's 2,711 headstones occupy an entire Berlin square – the determination to simultaneously keep memory alive and champion peace often draws its strength from the creation of a large empty space surrounded – or not – by remembrance walls formed in squares or circles, or planted shrubs. This approach can be seen in memorials such as the Memorial Plaza designed by landscape artist Peter Walker (b. 1932), which complements the enormous twin waterfall pools (in the voids left by the destruction) of architect Michael Arad's National September 11 Memorial (inaugurated 2011), in New York. Also adopted by Herbert Baker (1862–1946) for the Neuve-Chapelle Indian Memorial (1927) and by Bernard Desmoulin (b. 1953) for the Memorial to the Wars in Indochina in Fréjus (1983), the arrangement of walls of names and a walk delineating a central garden was simplified in The Ring of Remembrance at Notre-Dame-de-Lorette (2014), which bears the names of 579,606 soldiers from all countries (representing four nationalities), who were killed between 1914 and 1918 along the 90 kilometres of the Nord-Pas-de-Calais front. Its architect, Philippe Prost (b. 1959), explained: 'We wanted to give brotherhood a shape, convey an expression of peace, combine art with nature, to put them all at the service of memory.'

Today, along with places of remembrance and the institutional readings of history found in interpretation centres, gardens of peace are being rethought by gardeners, landscape architects and artists. Opportunities are provided by programmes such as the international landscape art project in the Hauts-de-France region and participative installations such as *Champs de Paix* (Fields of Peace) in Amiens's Saint-Pierre Park, created by landscape artist Béatrice Saurel in 2016 to commemorate the centennial of the Battle of the Somme and made with Amiens schoolchildren and retirement home residents. Today, this continues, thanks to passers-by who add scraps of clothing to the low horizontal ropes of the artwork as markers for their wishes for peace. Started by UNESCO and animated by a spirit of action for 'a culture of peace', these initiatives encourage the participation of a variety of social groups in remembrance, gardening and creation projects that bind together plant maintenance and the preservation of memory.[1]

To add to all these projects, we might add the soundscape invented by an Australian journalist Edward George Honey, who in May 1919 suggested to a London newspaper the observance of five minutes' silence in remembrance of the fallen of the

Ruins of the church at Ornes, a 'French village destroyed in the First World War', Verdun Forest, Meuse, 2019

The Garden of Exile of the Jewish Museum, Kreuzberg, Berlin, 2001 (architect: Daniel Libeskind)

First World War. In France, the first 'minute's silence' took place on 11 November 1922, four years after the Armistice, to indefatigably proclaim: 'Never again, Nimmermehr, Plus jamais!'[2] **M.R.**

---

1 UNESCO coordinated actions within the remit of the International Year for the Culture of Peace, which was designated by the United Nations as the year 2000.

2 See <https://www.franceculture.fr/societe/11-novembre-1922-la-premiere-minute-de-silence-de-france>. A 'minutes's silence' was a new form of commemoration in France, which came from the English tradition.

*Champs de Paix* (Fields of Peace), Saint-Pierre Park, Amiens, 2016 (landscape artist: Béatrice Saurel)

Hiroshima Peace Memorial Park, 1954 (architect: Kenzo Tange)

National September 11 Memorial & Museum, New York, 2011 and 2014 (architect: Michael Arad; landscape architect: Peter Walker)

# LANDSCAPES AND GARDENS OF PEACE

## Photographs by Christine Bastin and Jacques Evrard

*Soldiers' graves are the greatest preachers of peace.*
ALBERT SCHWEITZER (1875–1965),
awarded The Nobel Peace Prize 1952

Most people have seen or visited a war cemetery, sometimes even two or three … Yet we had to wait for the research and visual interpretation of Christine Bastin and Jacques Evrard to discover the many unknown roads linking the memorial sites of Belgium to those of the Hauts-de-France (France's northernmost region), and the battlefields of Normandy. Today we can at last visualise the manner in which each country honoured its fallen, with their invention of war cemeteries and memorials for the families of the fallen and for each of us. Although they might look like amalgamations of landscaping and architectural creations, when experienced as actual places these memorials encapsulate the intense emotions that shape a true heritage of consciousness. As Jacques Evrard often comments, 'Each time it's a shock.'

How are these places able to speak so intimately to their visitors? Why do families, friends and tourists feel such emotion? Maybe also because these cemeteries have their antecedents in previous civilian graveyards and in the gardening and landscaping traditions particular to each country. Why are the memorials respected to such an extent and how is it that they are so integral to the landscape of the local inhabitants? Perhaps because these places constantly nourish the emergence of projects honouring the countless dead and their underground presence. Indeed, fostered within the memory of each nation, these spaces testify to the horrors of war through the prism of a landscape of peace.

The major strands that are seen as part of the invention of a landscape of remembrance emerged along with other developments: the memory of the English garden in British creations; the cult of the forest in German graveyards; the staging of power in American cemeteries; the simplicity and purity of French cemeteries; the Allies' use of natural materials and animals to affirm the specificity of landscape, such as Canada's caribou, South Africa's common oak and Ireland's black granite …

Shedding light on the unknown landscaping, architectural and artistic qualities of these places, Bastin's and Evrard's images invite us to discover an initial inventory of these remembrance sites. Perhaps, one day, regional inventories and in-depth studies will complete their pioneering work. The broad range of images presented in this book allow us to compare the landscaping visions of each country's creators: they invite us to explore from various degrees of perception, from approaching a monument and observing its integration into the wider landscape, to viewing its surroundings, and to focusing on the borders, the threshold, the discovery of the garden-cemetery itself, its architecture, right down to the smallest details of remembrance art. **M.R.**

Normandy American Cemetery, Visitors' Centre (2007), Coleville-sur-Mer, Calvados, WW2
(architects: John Lampros and Nicolas Kelemen; landscape architects: D Paysage and Michael Vergason)

# GREAT LANDSCAPE

The photographic approach allows each garden cemetery to be put into context, in relation with its immediate environment and the landscape further away, which often consists of furrowed fields and rolling hills. Viewed like this, the landscape becomes a casket for the garden cemetery.

Bourdon German War Cemetery, Somme, WW2 (architect: Paul Schmitthenner)

Fleury-devant-Douaumont French National Cemetery, Meuse, WW1

Hartmannswillerkopf (Le Vieil Armand) French National Cemetery, Wattwiller, Haut-Rhin, WW1

American Military Cemetery and Memorial, Colleville-sur-Mer, Calvados, WW2 (landscape architects: Harbeson, Hough, Livingston & Larson; landscaping: Markley Stevenson)

View towards Omaha Beach, Normandy, WW2

Serre-Hébuterne French National Cemetery, Beaumont-Hamel, Somme, WW1

Somme American Cemetery and Memorial, Bony, Aisne, WW1

Montaigu I German War Cemetery, Aisne, WW1 (architect: Robert Tischler)

Pigeon Ravine British War Cemetery, Épehy, Somme, WW1 (architect: John Reginald Truelove)

Villers-Bretonneux British War Cemetery and Australian National Memorial, Somme, WW1 (architects: Edwin Lutyens and George H. Goldsmith)

Sir John Monash Centre, Villers-Bretonneux, Somme, WW1 (architects: Philip Cox and JLA)

Sainte-Croix-aux-Mines French National Cemetery, Haut-Rhin, WW1

Glorieux French National Cemetery, Verdun, Meuse, WW1

Marfaux British War Cemetery, Marne, WW1 (architect: Edwin Lutyens)

Bedford House British War Cemetery, Ypres, West Flanders, Belgium, WW1 (architect: Wilfred Clement von Berg)

Three of the British cemeteries in Beaumont-Hamel, Somme, WW1. Foreground: Beaumont-Hamel British Cemetery (architect: William Harrison Cowlishaw); background: Redan Ridge Cemetery No. 2; above: Redan Ridge Cemetery No. 1 (architect: Wilfred Clement von Berg)

# SURROUNDINGS

A memorial includes the impression experienced by visitors as they approach its surroundings via a path, a road, a field or even a communal graveyard. Its placement must be put on display in the same way as would be the case for a church or a natural site. At the same time, the remembrance setting must be protected while also leaving a sufficiently large field of visibility around the war cemetery, as is commonplace with other historic places.

Marfaux British War Cemetery, Marne, WW1 (architect: Edwin Lutyens)
Following pages:
Beaumetz-lès-Cambrai War Cemetery No. 1, Pas-de-Calais, WW1 (architect: Wilfred Clement von Berg)

Redan Ridge Cemetery No. 3, Beaumont-Hamel, Somme, WW1 (architect: Wilfred Clement von Berg)

Thilloy Road Cemetery, Beaulencourt, Pas-de-Calais, WW1 (architect: John Reginald Truelove)

Neuve-Chapelle Indian Memorial, Richebourg, Pas-de-Calais, WW1 (architect: Herbert Baker)

The Ring of Remembrance, Ablain-Saint-Nazaire French War Cemetery, Pas-de-Calais, WW1 (architect: Philippe Prost)

L'Orée de la Forêt French and German War Cemetery, Rossignol, Belgium, WW1 (architects: Henry Lacoste and Louis Madeline)

Pétant French National Cemetery, Montauville, Meurthe-et-Moselle, WW1 and WW2

Noyers-Pont-Maugis German War Cemetery, Ardennes, WW1 and WW2 (architect: Joseph Orth)

Bouillonville German War Cemetery, Meurthe-et-Moselle, WW1 (architect: Robert Tischler)

Following pages:
Veslud German War Cemetery, Aisne, WW1 (architect: Paul Scholzen)

# BORDERS

All war cemeteries are encircled by a boundary – most often a wall, sometimes a hedge – reminiscent of the Gallo-Roman *hortus gardinus*, the 'enclosed garden' sheltered from its environment, and the origin of the words 'garden' in English and '*jardin*' in French. Sufficiently low not to break the view but suitably tall to symbolically protect a place of contemplation, the shape of these walls recall those of orchards and kitchen gardens, although they are more elegant. They delineate the territory ceded to each nation entrusted with its responsibility.

Hooglede German War Cemetery, West Flanders, Belgium, WW1 (architect: Robert Tischler)

Cabaret-Rouge British Cemetery, Souchez, Pas-de-Calais, WW1 (architect: Frank Higginson)

Y Farm British War Cemetery, Bois-Grenier, Nord, WW1 (architect: Herbert Baker)

Shrine British War Cemetery, Bucquoy, Pas-de-Calais, WW1 (architect: William Harrison Cowlishaw)

Bény-sur-Mer Canadian War Cemetery, Reviers, Calvados, WW2 (architect: Philip Hepworth)

Trefcon British Cemetery, Aisne, WW1 and WW2 (architect: Charles Henry Holden)

Louverval British War Cemetery, Doignies, Nord, WW1

Lichfield Crater British Cemetery and Memorial, Thélus, Pas-de-Calais, WW1 (architect: William Harrison Cowlishaw)

British War Cemetery, Corbie Communal Cemetery Extension, Somme, WW1 (architects: Charles Henry Holden and William Harrison Cowlishaw)

# THRESHOLDS

Like the limits of a garden, the threshold of the war cemetery instantly reveals the soul of the place through both its general presentation and its details. A few meticulously cut stones, a little bridge, a large slab, or a gateway with its carefully designed latch, a reception centre sheltering visitors from the wind and the rain – every detail of the threshold is unveiled like a courtesy to the visitor and represents another homage to the soldiers whose bodies lie beyond.

Montay-Neuvilly Road British War Cemetery, Nord, WW1 (architects: Charles Henry Holden and William Harrison Cowlishaw)

La Cambe German War Cemetery, Calvados, WW2 (architect: Robert Tischler)

'Studentenfriedhof' German War Cemetery, Langemark, West Flanders, Belgium, WW1 (architect: Robert Tischler)

V.C. Corner Australian Cemetery, Fromelles, Nord, WW1 (architects: Herbert Baker and William Harrison Cowlishaw)

Rossignol Plateau French–German War Cemetery, Tintigny, Luxembourg, Belgium, WW1 (architect: Ludwig Paffendorf)

Le Trou Aid Post British War Cemetery, Fleurbaix, Pas-de-Calais, WW1 (architects: Herbert Baker and John Reginald Truelove)

Gorre British and Indian Cemetery, Beuvry, Pas-de-Calais, WW1 (architects: Charles Henry Holden and Wilfred Clement von Berg)

Ethe Laclaireau French War Cemetery, Luxembourg, Belgium, WW1

Longuyon German War Cemetery, Meurthe-et-Moselle, WW1 (architect: Robert Tischler)

Lissey German War Cemetery, Meuse, WW1 (architect: Robert Tischler)

Ontario Cemetery, Sains-lès-Marquion, Pas-de-Calais, WW1 (architects: Edwin Lutyens and Noel Ackroyd Rew)

Soupir French National Cemetery No. 1, Aisne, WW1

Urville Polish War Cemetery, Grainville-Langannerie, Calvados, WW2 (architect: Pierre Bienvenu; sculptors: Charles Gianferrari and Jacques Bertoux)

Richebourg Portuguese War Cemetery, Pas-de-Calais, WW1

Schaeferthal Romanian War Cemetery, Soultzmatt, Haut-Rhin, WW1

Rossignol Plateau French Military Cemetery, Luxembourg, Belgium, WW1

Hooge Crater War Cemetery, Zillebeke (Ypres), West Flanders, Belgium, WW1 (architects: Edwin Lutyens and Noel Ackroyd Rew)

Delville Wood South African National Memorial, Longueval, Somme, WW1 (architect: Herbert Baker)

La Targette French National Cemetery, Neuville-Saint-Vaast, Pas-de-Calais, WW1

Route de Solesmes German War Cemetery, Cambrai, Nord, WW1 (architect: Wilhelm Kreis)

Brussels War Cemetery, Field of Honour and Monumental Portal, Evere, WW1 (architect: François Malfait; sculptor: Mathieu Desmaré)

# GARDENS

The symbiosis between architects, landscape gardeners and horticulturists has rarely been deeper. The chosen planting usually draws its inspiration from its natural site or from the homeland of the men who rest there.

In order to affirm humankind's attachment to the memory of its fallen with the passing of the seasons, the maintenance of the garden demands a multitude of gardeners.

The cultivation and maintenance of the plants, steps, benches and pergolas become marks of respect that are paced according to the constant rhythm of plants, seasons and the passage of visitors.

Stump Road British War Cemetery, Grandcourt, Somme, WW1
(architects: Herbert Baker and Arthur James Scott Hutton)

Neuville-Saint-Vaast German War Cemetery, Pas-de-Calais, WW1 (architect: Joseph Orth)

Saint-Symphorien British War Cemetery, Hainaut, Belgium, WW1 (architect: William Harrison Cowlishaw)

Buttes New British War Cemetery, Zonnebeke, West Flanders, Belgium, WW1 (architect: Charles Henry Holden)

Lorraine American Cemetery and Memorial, Saint-Avold, Moselle, WW2 (architects: Murphy & Locraft ; landscape architect: Allyn R. Jennings of Oley)

‘Studentenfriedhof’ German War Cemetery, Langemark, West Flanders, Belgium, WW1 (architect: Robert Tischler)

Lissey German War Cemetery, Meuse, WW1 (architect: Robert Tischler)

Bourdon German War Cemetery, Somme, WW2 (architect: Paul Schmitthenner)

Nolette Chinese Cemetery, Noyelles-sur-Mer, Somme, WW1 (architects: Edwin Lutyens and John Reginald Truelove)

La Cambe German War Cemetery, Calvados, WW2 (architect: Robert Tischler)

Henri-Chapelle American Cemetery and Memorial, Liège, Belgium, WW2 (architects: Holabird, Root & Burgee; landscape architect: Franz Lipp)

La Cambe German War Cemetery, Calvados, WW2 (architect: Robert Tischler)

Soupir German War Cemetery, Aisne, WW1 (architect: Robert Tischler)

Sainte-Marie-aux-Mines 'Montgoutte' German War Cemetery, Haut-Rhin, WW1 (architect: Robert Tischler)

Noyers-Pont-Maugis German War Cemetery, Ardennes, WW1 and WW2 (architect: Joseph Orth)

Hooglede German War Cemetery, West Flanders, Belgium, WW1 (architect: Robert Tischler)

Cabaret-Rouge British Cemetery, Souchez, Pas-de-Calais, WW1 (architect: Frank Higginson)

Cabaret-Rouge British Cemetery, Souchez, Pas-de-Calais, WW1 (architect: Frank Higginson)

Nolette Chinese Cemetery, Noyelles-sur-Mer, Somme, WW1 (architects: Edwin Lutyens and John Reginald Truelove)

Ryes British War Cemetery, Bazenville, Calvados, WW2 (architect: Philip Hepworth)

Bedford House British War Cemetery, Ypres, West Flanders, Belgium, WW1 (architect: Wilfred Clement von Berg)

Robermont German War Cemetery, Liège, Belgium, WW1 (architect: Emil Högg)

Warlincourt Halte British War Cemetery, Saulty, Pas-de-Calais, WW1 (architects: Charles Henry Holden and William Harrison Cowlishaw)

Tintigny/Bellefontaine French–German War Cemetery, Luxembourg, Belgium, WW1 (architect: Ludwig Paffendorf)

Saint-Symphorien German War Cemetery, Hainaut, Belgium, WW1 (architect: Robert Tischler)

Auvelais French War Cemetery, Namur, Belgium, WW1

‘Military square’ of Robermont Cemetery, Liège, Belgium, WW1 (architect: Victor Rogister)

Messines Ridge British War Cemetery, Ypres, West Flanders, Belgium, WW1 (architects: Charles Henry Holden and Wilfred Clement von Berg)

Pierrepont French National Cemetery, Meurthe-et-Moselle, WW1

Marchovelette Belgian War Cemetery, Champion, Namur, Belgium, WW1

Chambière French National Cemetery, Metz, Moselle, 1870 and WW1

Ayette Indian and Chinese Cemetery, Pas-de-Calais, WW1 (architect: William Harrison Cowlishaw)

Serre Road British Cemetery, Beaumont-Hamel, Somme, WW1

Cerny-en-Laonnois French National Cemetery, Aisne, WW1

Bény-sur-Mer Canadian War Cemetery, Reviers, Calvados, WW2 (architect: Philip Hepworth)

Buttes New British War Cemetery, Zonnebeke, West Flanders, Belgium, WW1 (architect: Charles Henry Holden)

Étaples British War Cemetery, Pas-de-Calais, WW1 (architects: Edwin Lutyens and George H. Goldsmith)

Normandy American War Cemetery and Memorial, Colleville-sur-Mer, Calvados, WW2 (landscape architects: Harbeson, Hough, Livingston & Larson; landscaping: Markley Stevenson)

Romagne-sous-Montfaucon American War Cemetery, Meuse, WW1 (architects: Louis Ayers and George Gibbs Jr; designer: York & Sawyer)

Garden of remembrance, Bligny Italian War Cemetery, Chambrecy, Marne, WW1

Brittany American War Cemetery, Montjoie-Saint-Martin, Manche, WW2 (architect: William T. Aldrich; landscaping: Shurcliff & Shurcliff)

Romagne-sous-Montfaucon American War Cemetery, Meuse, WW1 (architects: Louis Ayers and George Gibbs Jr; designer: York & Sawyer)

La Targette French National Cemetery, Neuville-Saint-Vaast, Pas-de-Calais, WW1

Bény-sur-Mer Canadian War Cemetery, Reviers, Calvados, WW2 (architect: Philip Hepworth)

Lorraine American Cemetery and Memorial, Saint-Avold, Moselle, WW2 (architects: Murphy & Locraft ; landscape architect: Allyn R. Jennings of Oley)

Tyne Cot Commonwealth War Graves Cemetery and Memorial to the Missing,
Zonnebeke, West Flanders, Belgium, WW1
(architects: Herbert Baker and John Reginald Truelove; sculptors: Joseph Armitage and Ferdinand Victor Blundstone)

Following pages:
Lorraine American Cemetery and Memorial, Saint-Avold, Moselle, WW2

# ARCHITECTURES AND MEMORIAL ART

It quickly became clear that to define a transition between place of meditation and living space, between nature and human architecture, small modest structures had to be erected to allow visitors and family members to find a comforting shelter away from the world, where they could contemplate, meditate and pray if they desired, and look for a name in the register and burial records. In designing elements such as headstones, crosses, altars, inscriptions, registers, ironwork, woodwork and stained glass, all participating artists and architects collaborated in the project in order to offer visitors work that is remarkable for its stylistic unity.

Dud Corner British War Cemetery and the Loos Memorial, Loos-en-Gohelle, Pas-de-Calais, WW1 (architect: Herbert Baker)

Henri-Chapelle American Cemetery and Memorial, Liège, Belgium, WW2
(architects: Holabird, Root & Burgee; landscape architect: Franz Lipp)

FERDINAND EPPSTEIN
ALBERT A. HARRIS

Vendresse British War Cemetery, Vendresse-Beaulne, Aisne, WW1 (architects: Edwin Lutyens and John Reginald Truelove)

Bretteville-sur-Laize Canadian War Cemetery, Cintheaux, Calvados, WW2 (architect: Philip Hepworth)

Noyers-Pont-Maugis German War Cemetery, Ardennes, WW1 and WW2 (architect: Joseph Orth)

Noyers-Pont-Maugis German War Cemetery, Ardennes, WW1 and WW2 (architect: Joseph Orth)

Montaigu I German War Cemetery, Aisne, WW1 (architect: Robert Tischler)

Montaigu I German War Cemetery, Aisne, WW1 (architect: Robert Tischler)

Bény-sur-Mer Canadian War Cemetery, Reviers, Calvados, WW2 (architect: Philip Hepworth)

Bourdon German War Cemetery, Somme, WW2 (architect: Paul Schmitthenner)

Bretteville-sur-Laize Canadian War Cemetery, Cintheaux, Calvados, WW2 (architect: Philip Hepworth)

Neuve-Chapelle Indian Memorial, Richebourg, Pas-de-Calais, WW1 (architect: Herbert Baker)

Montaigu I German War Cemetery, Aisne, WW1 (architect: Robert Tischler)

Louverval British War Cemetery and the Cambrai Memorial, Doignies, Nord, WW1 (architect: Harold Charlton Bradshaw)

Dud Corner British War Cemetery and the Loos Memorial, Loos-en-Gohelle, Pas-de-Calais, WW1 (architect: Herbert Baker)

Register at the Sains-lès-Marquion British 'Quarry Wood Cemetery', Pas-de-Calais, WW1 (architects: Edwin Lutyens and Noel Ackroyd Rew)

Register at the Cerny-en-Laonnois French National Cemetery, Aisne, WW1

Register at the Montaigu I German War Cemetery, Aisne, WW1 (architect: Robert Tischler)

Dud Corner British War Cemetery and the Loos Memorial, Loos-en-Gohelle, Pas-de-Calais, WW1 (architect: Herbert Baker)

Villers-Bretonneux British War Cemetery and Australian National Memorial, Somme, WW1 (architects: Edwin Lutyens and George H. Goldsmith)

Le Cateau German War Cemetery, Le Cateau-Cambrésis Nord, WW1 (architect: Robert Tischler)
Right: ‘Studentenfriedhof’ German War Cemetery, Langemark, West Flanders, Belgium, WW1 (architect: Robert Tischler)

DOEHLA EDUARD MAJOR † 14.4.1918 · DÖHLER KURT SOLDAT † 13.4.1917 · DÖHR ERICH MUSKETIER † 31.7.1917 · DÖLL KARL GEFREITER
† 9.10.1917 · DÖLLE ALEXANDER SCHÜTZE † 29.10.1918 · DÖLLE FRIEDRICH KRANKENTRÄGER † 8.11.1918 · DÖMLING HUGO INFANTERIST
† 30.10.1914 · DÖNEBEIN HANS UNTEROFFIZIER † 1915 · DÖNGES EWALD UNTEROFFIZIER † 4.10.1917 · DÖPFNER LUDWIG INFANTERIST † 2.11.1914
DÖPPENBECKER DIETRICH UNTEROFFIZIER † 13.9.1918 · DÖPPERT GEORG ERSATZ-RESERVIST † 13.11.1914 · DÖPPERT HEINRICH ERSATZ-
RESERVIST † 2.12.1914 · DÖPPL KARL INFANTERIST † 9.10.1917 · DÖRFLER ADOLF MUSKETIER † 17.5.1915 · DÖRFLER FRANZ KARL † 26.10.1917
DÖRFLER GEORG INFANTERIST † 31.7.1917 · DÖRFLER GEORG KRIEGSFREIWILLIGER † 2.11.1914 · DÖRFLER JAKOB INFANTERIST † 4.10.1917
DÖRFLER JOHANN INFANTERIST † 20.9.1917 · DÖRFLER JOHANN INFANTERIST † 26.10.1917 · DÖRFLER LUDWIG FELDWEBELLEUTNANT
† 29.10.1914 · DÖRFLINGER ERNST UNTEROFFIZIER † 31.10.1914 · DOERING FERDINAND LEUTNANT † 2.11.1914 · DÖOLING EWALD RESERVIST
† 2.2.1915 · DÖRING ADAM WEHRMANN † 8.11.1914 · DÖRING AUGUST ERSATZ-RESERVIST † 26.7.1915 · DÖRING GUSTAV WEHRMANN † 10.11.1914
DÖRING KLEMENS RESERVIST † 10.11.1914 · DÖRING MAX OBERMATROSE † 31.10.1918 · DÖRLL HEINRICH † 16.6.1915 · DÖRNBRACK JOHANN
GEFREITER † 6.8.1914 · DÖRRIES KARL JÄGER † 24.4.1915 · DÖSCHER HERMANN VIZEFELDWEBEL † 26.9.1917 · DÖSS WILHELM ERSATZ-RESERVIST
† 24.5.1915 · DÖTTLING HERMANN GEFREITER † 1.11.1914 · DOHMEN PETER GARDIST † 26.9.1917 · DOHMS KARL MUSKETIER † 4.10.1917 · DOHRMANN
GUSTAV FÜSILIER † 26.8.1914 · DOHRMANN MICHAEL ERSATZ-RESERVIST † 19.11.1919 · DOHRN KARL † 21.10.1918 · DOLATOWSKI XAVER
MUSKETIER † 6.8.1914 · DOLD HERMANN † 13.11.1914 · DOLD REINHARD RESERVIST † 21.2.1915 · DOLDASINSKI JOSEF GEFREITER † 26.10.1918
DOLDERER MEINRAD RESERVIST † 9.5.1915 · DOLL BERNHARD HORNIST † 29.4.1915 · DOLL CHRISTIAN GEFREITER † 22.8.1914 · DOLL GEORG
INFANTERIST † 27.4.1918 · DOLL JOHANN INFANTERIST † 29.10.1914 · DOLL JOHANNES ERSATZ-RESERVIST † 8.5.1915 · DOLL WILHELM
LANDSTURMMANN † 12.10.1917 · DOLLESCHEL EDUARD INFANTERIST † 29.10.1914 · DOMAGALSKI LORENZ GEFREITER † 24.8.1917 · DOMANETZKI
ALFRED LEUTNANT † 28.10.1918 · DOMBECK PETER MUSKETIER † 7.11.1918 · DOMEN KARL † 20.4.1918 · DOMHARDT OTTO LANDSTURMMANN
† 11.6.1916 · DOMIS FRANZ GEFREITER † 9.12.1914 · DOMKE GERHARD GEFREITER † 26.9.1917 · DOMKE WALTER JÄGER † 12.10.1917 · DOMPERT
WILHELM WEHRMANN † 26.10.1914 · DONEYER FRIEDRICH RESERVIST † 16.3.1915 · DONGES HEINRICH JÄGER † 25.10.1918 · DONHAUSER JOHANN
INFANTERIST † 10.11.1914 · DONNERSTAG PAUL KANONIER † 4.10.1918 · DONWARTH LUDWIG † 15.5.1915 · DOPIRALA FRANZ MUSKETIER † 26.4.1918
DOPPMANN BERNHARD UNTEROFFIZIER † 4.10.1917 · DORBERTH ADAM INFANTERIST † 16.8.1917 · DORFF HERMANN UNTEROFFIZIER † 7.11.1914
DORGE PAUL GEFREITER † 4.10.1917 · DORMANN FRANZ INFANTERIST † 29.3.1915 · DORMANN HEINRICH MUSKETIER † 29.5.1918 · DORMANN
JOHANN INFANTERIST † 7.6.1917 · DORN JOHANN GEFREITER † 4.11.1914 · DORN JOSEF MUSKETIER † 10.5.1915 · DORNAUER ADAM INFANTERIST
† 3.11.1914 · DORNER HANS INFANTERIST † 9.10.1917 · DOROW MAX VIZEFELDWEBEL † 22.8.1914 · DORSCH PAUL MUSKETIER † 17.1.1918 · DORSCHEL
JOHANN † 9.10.1917 · DORSZ BOLESLAUS MUSKETIER † 4.10.1917 · DOSCH CLEMENS INFANTERIST † 8.11.1914 · DOSIG ROBERT LANDSTURMMANN
† 15.10.1918 · DOSS PAUL KANONIER † 25.10.1918 · DOSTALL OTTO OBERMATROSE † 1.10.1918 · DOTTERWEICH GEORG GEFREITER † 11.9.1917
DOUGA STANISLAUS WEHRMANN † 10.11.1914 · DRÄGER FERDINAND LANDSTURMMANN † 19.10.1915 · DRÄGER FRITZ SCHÜTZE † 4.10.1917
DRÄGER GUSTAV · DRAGMANN · DRECHSEL FRANZ SOLDAT † 19.3.1915 · DRECHSEL GEORG INFANTERIST † 9.6.1917 · DRECHSLER JOHANN
GEFREITER † 17.3.1917 · DRECHSLER JOSEF LANDSTURMMANN † 17.11.1914 · DRECKSTRATER ERICH · DREES ANTON MUSKETIER † 6.8.1914
DREGER BERTHOLD LANDSTURMMANN † 26.9.1917 · DREHER EDMUND MUSKETIER † 24.8.1917 · DREHER EDUARD LANDSTURMREKRUT † 4.10.1917
DREHER KARL ERSATZ-RESERVIST † 12.11.1914 · DREIER FRANZ GEFREITER † 20.9.1917 · DREILICH FRIEDRICH RESERVIST † 22.8.1914 · DREISING
NIKOLAUS SCHÜTZE † 14.10.1918 · DREISING WOLFGANG † 26.4.1915 · DREISSIG ERICH PIONIER † 13.11.1918 · DREISSIG REINHOLD SERGEANT
† 29.10.1918 · DREIST OTTO GEFREITER † 28.10.1918 · DREITTINGER JOHANN INFANTERIST † 29.10.1914 · DRENKHAHN HERMANN UNTEROFFIZIER
† 24.8.1914 · DRENS OTTO · DRESCH FRANZ INFANTERIST † 9.11.1914 · DRESCH JAKOB INFANTERIST † 31.1.1915 · DRESCHER ERHARD GEFREITER
† 16.8.1917 · DRESCHER GUSTAV INFANTERIST † 8.11.1914 · DRESCHER JOSEF MUSKETIER † 31.1.1917 · DRESCHER WILLY SOLDAT † 17.1.1915
DRESE OSWALD LANDSTURMREKRUT † 15.6.1917 · DRESEN WILHELM UNTEROFFIZIER † 8.11.1914 · DRESSEL KARL INFANTERIST † 1.12.1914
DRESSEL RUDOLF JÄGER † 4.11.1914 · DRESSEN MATHIAS MUSKETIER † 15.11.1917 · DRESSLER EUGEN RESERVIST † 26.8.1914 · DREWES GUSTAV
GEFREITER † 20.9.1917 · DREWES HEINRICH PIONIER † 17.9.1918 · DREWS ANDREAS GEFREITER † 8.11.1918 · DREXL HEINRICH GEFREITER
† 8.10.1917 · DREXLER WILHELM ERSATZ-RESERVIST † 8.11.1914 · DREYER FRITZ SCHÜTZE † 13.11.1918 · DREYER LEOPOLD KRANKENTRÄGER
† 26.8.1914 · DRIGALLE GUSTAV WEHRMANN † 7.11.1914 · DRISCHMANN WILHELM SERGEANT † 16.8.1917 · DRISSLER FRANZ INFANTERIST
† 17.11.1914 · DROBOT HEINRICH WEHRMANN † 4.11.1914 · DRÖGE AUGUST MUSKETIER † 8.11.1918 · DRÖGEMÜLLER OTTO UNTEROFFIZIER
† 8.11.1918 · DRÖNLE JOSEF MUSKETIER † 23.8.1914 · DROSE AUGUST RESERVIST † 5.11.1914 · DROSTE FRITZ GEFREITER † 9.11.1914 · DRUCK
EUGEN INFANTERIST † 29.4.1918 · DRUCK JOHANN INFANTERIST † 11.11.1914 · DRUCK JOHANNES WEHRMANN † 8.11.1914 · DRUCKENBROD EMIL
INFANTERIST † 27.10.1917 · DRUM LUDWIG INFANTERIST † 17.11.1914 · DRUMM KARL LANDSTURMMANN † 7.6.1917 · DRUSCHBA FRANZ GEFREITER
† 4.10.1917 · DRZYMALA PETER GEFREITER † 10.11.1914 · DUBBELFELD PETER GRENADIER † 17.4.1918 · DUCKHORN PAUL WEHRMANN † 16.11.1914
DUDA ANDREAS RESERVIST † 22.8.1914 · DUDALSKI JOSEF KRIEGSFREIWILLIGER † 13.1.1915 · DUDSZUS KARL FÜSILIER † 27.9.1917 · DÜBLER MAX
MUSKETIER † 22.8.1914 · DÜLL PAUL MUSKETIER † 22.8.1914 · DÜLPERT NIKOLAUS INFANTERIST † 16.8.1917 · DÜM JOHANN INFANTERIST
† 27.10.1917 · DÜMMLER KARL VIZEFELDWEBEL † 18.10.1917 · DÜMMLER KONRAD KRANKENTRÄGER † 3.11.1917 · DÜMPELMANN FRANZ WEHRMANN
† 20.9.1917 · DÜNKELMANN GUSTAV GEFREITER † 27.11.1916 · DÜNZINGER JOSEPH RESERVIST † 10.3.1915 · DÜRENFELD GUSTAV WEHRMANN
† 7.11.1914 · DÜRING ADOLF UNTEROFFIZIER † 12.11.1914 · DÜRING KARL VIZEFELDWEBEL † 30.9.1917 · DÜRR BERNHARD RESERVIST † 23.9.1914
DÜRR ERNST LEUTNANT † 24.10.1914 · DÜRR GEORG INFANTERIST † 5.11.1914 · DÜRR GUSTAV KRIEGSFREIWILLIGER · DÜRR JOHANN ERSATZ-
RESERVIST † 8.6.1917 · DÜRR JOHANN INFANTERIST † 27.5.1918 · DÜRR JOHANN LANDSTURMMANN † 21.7.1917 · DÜRR MATTHIAS GEFREITER
† 29.10.1914 · DÜRRENBERGER JOSEF KRIEGSFREIWILLIGER † 13.5.1915 · DÜRRSCHMIDT JOHANN UNTEROFFIZIER † 17.4.1918 · DÜSEL HEINRICH
INFANTERIST † 3.11.1914 · DÜTSCH MICHAEL INFANTERIST † 18.11.1914 · DÜVIER FRANZ WEHRMANN † 20.7.1915 · DÜWEL WILHELM MUSKETIER
† 4.10.1917 · DÜWERT KARL LANDSTURMREKRUT † 2.6.1915 · DUFOUR EMIL LANDSTURMMANN † 24.5.1918 · DUHN MUSKETIER · DUIN WALTER
† 2.8.1915 · DUMSKY JOHANN ERSATZ-RESERVIST † 20.9.1917 · DUNKA RICHARD MUSKETIER † 11.11.1914 · DUNKEN ERNST JÄGER † 12.10.1917
DUNKER HEINRICH WEHRMANN † 10.11.1914 · DUNSE EHRHARD UNTEROFFIZIER † 28.10.1918 · DUNSINGER HEINRICH UNTEROFFIZIER † 3.2.1915
DUNZ HERMANN SERGEANT † 6.11.1918 · DUPPE JOHANN INFANTERIST † 14.3.1915 · DURCHHOLZ AUGUST GEFREITER † 2.11.1914 · DURST ANTON
GEFREITER † 20.9.1917 · DURST EUGEN UNTEROFFIZIER † 16.6.1915 · DURST GEORG INFANTERIST † 4.10.1917 · DURSY OTTO ERSATZ-RESERVIST
† 13.10.1917 · DURTEL OTTO KANONIER † 22.10.1918 · DUSCHA VIKTOR UNTEROFFIZIER † 17.8.1917 · DUTSCHKE PAUL GRENADIER † 11.11.1914
DUTTENHÖFER RICHARD INFANTERIST † 1.9.1915 · DUTTINE PHILIPP INFANTERIST † 4.10.1917 · DUWERT RICHARD WEHRMANN † 7.11.1914
DYBIONA MARTIN GEFREITER † 7.11.1914 · DYCK ALFRED OFFIZIERSSTELLVERTRETER † 2.11.1914 · DYMKE ALFRED MUSKETIER † 3.12.1917
DYROFF ADAM INFANTERIST † 15.11.1914 · DZIALAS KARL LEUTNANT † 25.10.1918 · DZIOBAKA ADOLF LANDSTURMMANN † 10.8.1917

Laeken Cemetery, Brussels, WW1

Honnechy British War Cemetery, Nord, WW1 (architects: Charles Henry Holden and Wilfred Clement von Berg)

COURSQUER
CREMAULT MAXIME
CHASSANAN
TRISGARLEN
HUPSKI W.A.
WJERSCHONIN IVAN
SOLDAT RUSSE
MORT POUR LA FRANCE le 27-12-1944
LOZBENEY C.
SOLDAT RUSSE
MORT POUR LA FRANCE le 20-3-1945

Thiaucourt-Regniéville German War Cemetery, Meurthe-et-Moselle, 1870–71 and WW1
Left: Pétant French National Cemetery, Montauville, Meurthe-et-Moselle, WW1 and WW2

Mont-de-Huisnes German War Cemetery Mausoleum, Manche, WW2 (architect: Johannes Krahn)

Henri-Chapelle American Cemetery and Memorial, Liège, Belgium, WW2 (architects: Holabird, Root & Burgee; landscape archtect: Franz Lipp)

Pétant French National Cemetery, Montauville, Meurthe-et-Moselle, WW1 and WW2

Saint-Étienne-au-Mont Chinese War Cemetery, Pas-de-Calais, WW1

Saint-Mihiel American War Cemetery and Memorial, Thiaucourt-Regniéville, Meurthe-et-Moselle, WW1 (architect: Thomas Harlan Ellett)

Sillery French National Cemetery, Marne, WW1 (architect: Adolphe Prost; sculptors: Édouard Sediey, Berton, Lacote and Pellue)

Noyers-Pont-Maugis German War Cemetery, Ardennes, WW1 and WW2 (architect: Joseph Orth)

Neuville-en-Condroz 'Ardennes American Cemetery', Neupré, Liège, Belgium, WW2

# MEMORIALS

Recording the names of the dead who had no graves and registering them on a memorial did not start until late 1918, as people wanted to include the names of the places where the fallen had supposedly died. This wish determined the nature of many future projects, evolving over time and with the rhythm of wars, ranging from grandiose upright memorials to the more modest remembrance gardens.

Thiepval Memorial to the Missing of the Somme, WW1 (architect: Edwin Lutyens)

Beaumont-Hamel Newfoundland Memorial (The Caribou), Somme, WW1 (architect: Rudolf Cochius; sculptor: Basil Gotto)

9th Scottish Division Memorial, Athies, Pas-de-Calais, WW1

Malmedy American Memorial, Baugnez, Liège, Belgium, WW2 (architect: Roger Bastin)

Malmedy American Memorial, Baugnez, Liège, Belgium, WW2 (architect: Roger Bastin)

Vis-en-Artois British Cemetery and Memorial, Haucourt, Pas-de-Calais, WW1 (architect: John Reginald Truelove)

Faubourg d'Amiens British Cemetery and The Arras Memorial, Arras, Pas-de-Calais, WW1 (architect: Edwin Lutyens; sculptor: William Reid Dick)

Right and following pages:
Canadian National Vimy Memorial, Givenchy-en-Gohelle, Pas-de-Calais, WW1 (architect and sculptor: Walter Seymour Allward)

Villers-Bretonneux British War Cemetery and Australian National Memorial, Somme, WW1 (architects: Edwin Lutyens and George H. Goldsmith)
Le Cateau German War Cemetery, Le Cateau-Cambrésis Nord, WW1 (architect: Robert Tischler)

Neuville-Saint-Vaast Memorial to the Czech Volunteers, Pas-de-Calais, WW1 and WW2

Flanders Field American Cemetery and Memorial, Waregem, West Flanders, Belgium, WW1 (architect: Paul P. Cret; landscape architect: Jacques Greber)

Island of Ireland Peace Park, Messines, West Flanders, Belgium, WW1 (architects: O'Gram, Toone Breys)

Romagne-sous-Montfaucon American Memorial, Meuse, WW1
(architect: John Russell Pope)

Sillery French National Cemetery, Marne, WW1
(architect: Adolphe Prost; sculptors: Édouard Sediey, Berton, Lacote and Pellue)

National Deportation Memorial, Natzweiler-Struthof concentration camp, Natzwiller, Bas-Rhin, WW2 (architect: Bertrand Monnet)

Delville Wood South African National Memorial, Longueval, Somme, WW1 (architect: Herbert Baker)

The Ring of Remembrance, Ablain-Saint-Nazaire French War Cemetery, Pas-de-Calais, WW1 (architect: Philippe Prost)

Hartmannswillerkopf (Le Vieil Armand) French National Monument, Wattwiller, Haut-Rhin, WW1
(architect: Robert Danis; restoration: Michel Spitz)

## ABOUT THE AUTHORS

**Christine Bastin and Jacques Evrard**
This team of photographers have conceived, individually and together, over 40 books about architecture – from eclecticism to Art Nouveau, from Art Deco to contemporary works – as well as books about gardens and landscape art. They have participated in many exhibitions in Belgium, France, Germany, Spain, Italy, Japan and the United States, notably *Jardins des plaisirs* in collaboration with the author and musicologist Gérard Gefen. In 2008, *L'eau dans les jardins d'Europe*, which they created in partnership with the historian Michel Baridon, was awarded the René Pechère Prize and the Prix Redouté (historical category). Bastin and Evrard photographed the images included in *Gardens of Peace* between 2014 and 2019.

**Marie-Madeleine Damien**
Associate Professor Emeritus at the University of Lille, Marie-Madeleine Damien directed the 'Planning, heritage and tourist appreciation' masters programme from 1996 to 2014. With the help of her students, she conducted an outline inventory of the remains of First World War funeral sites and memorials in the Hauts-de-France region. She is Secretary General of the Paysages et Sites de mémoire de la Grande Guerre association.

**Paul Gough**
Painter, broadcaster and academic, Paul Gough has exhibited his paintings around the world and is represented in various permanent collections, including London's Imperial War Museum, Ottawa's Canadian War Museum and Wellington's National War Memorial. His research on conflict and peace has been presented at many conferences, symposiums and exhibitions, and he has published several books on the iconography of commemoration. Gough is Pro Vice-Chancellor and Vice-President at the College of Design and Social Context, RMIT University, Melbourne, Australia.

**Bernard Klein**
After having gained a master's degree in history and human resources at the University of Strasbourg, Bernard Klein headed the human resources departments of several companies in France and Germany. Since 1995 he has directed the International Youth Centre Albert Schweitzer in Niederbronn-les-Bains in the Alsace region, a project financed by the German War Graves Commission.

**Isabelle Loodts**
Isabelle Loodts once worked as an archaeologist of prehistory, but ten years ago she turned her back on the Neanderthal to concentrate on the remains of the First World War. Her investigation into the environmental consequences of the conflict is based on her ongoing 'Landscapes at War' documentary project. The independent journalist writes numerous articles for the press and reports for both radio and television.

**Chantal Pradines**
A specialist of tree avenues and the author of several studies, including the 'Infrastructures routières: les allées d'arbres dans le paysage' report for the Council of Europe in 2009, in 2018 Chantal Pradines organised the international 'Tree avenues – from war to peace' symposium, which explored the subject of memorial avenues planted during and after the First World War.

**Michel Racine**
Architect and garden urban planner, adviser for the development of the landscape for tourists, author of the first regional inventory of gardens in France (1983) and of more than 20 books on dwellings, gardens and their creators, Michel Racine is Member of Honour of the ICOMOS-IFLA International Scientific Committee on Cultural Landscapes. He has also lectured at Versailles' École Nationale Supérieure de Paysage, initiated the '*Visitez un jardin en France*' campaign (ARPEJ, 1987) and the opening of the King's Kitchen Garden at Versailles to the public (1992), and has founded several other associations promoting healing gardens.

**Simon Rietz**
Landscape architect Simon Rietz is the author of a study on landscape and open space planning and another on renewable energies and raw materials. His doctorate focused on the history of First World War German war cemeteries. Today he works in the area of regional development of the German–Danish coast in the North Sea.

## SELECTED BIBLIOGRAPHY


André, Édouard, 1879, *L'Art des jardins* (Paris: Masson)

Arendt, Max, 1935, 'Die Bauten des Volksbundes in ihrer geschichtlichen und kulturellen Bedeutung', *Kriegsgräberfürsorge* 2, pp. 19–24

Ariès, Philippe, 1975, *Essais sur l'histoire de la mort en Occident, du Moyen Âge à nos jours* (Paris: Éditions du Seuil)

— 1977, *L'homme devant la mort: I. Le temps des gisants; II. La mort ensauvagée* (Paris: Éditions du Seuil)

Auzelle, Robert, 1965, *Dernières demeures: Conception, composition, réalisation du cimetière contemporain*, drawings by Dominique Jankovic (Paris: Imprimerie Mazarine)

Basu, Paul, 2007, 'Palimpsest Memoryscapes: Materializing and Mediating War and Peace in Sierra Leone', in Ferdinand de Jong and Michael Rowlands (eds), *Reclaiming Heritage: Alternative Imaginaries of Memory in West Africa* (Walnut Creek, CA: Left Coast Press), pp. 231–59

Bellanger, Emmanuel, and Danielle Tartakowsky (eds), 2011, *Cimetières et politique* issue of *Le Mouvement social* 4/237

Belmas, Élisabeth, and Serenella Nonnis-Vigilante (eds), 2017, *L'orchestration de la mort: Les funérailles, des temps modernes à l'époque contemporaine* (Villeneuve-d'Ascq: Presses universitaires du Septentrion)

Bender, Barbara (ed.), 1983, *Landscape: Politics and Perspectives* (Oxford: Berg)

Bender, Barbara, and Margot Winer (eds), 2001, *Contested Landscapes: Movement, Exile and Place* (Oxford: Berg)

Bertrand, Régis, and Anne Carol (eds), 2016, *Aux origines des cimetières contemporains: Les réformes funéraires de l'Europe occidentale, XVIIIe–XIXe siècle* (Aix-en-Provence: Presses universitaires de Provence)

Beveridge, Charles E., and Paul Rocheleau, 1998, *Frederick Law Olmsted: Designing the American Landscape* (New York: Universe)

Biraben, Anne, 1995, *Les cimetières militaires*

*en France, Architecture et paysage* (Paris: L'Harmattan)
Blackett, Heather, 1986, 'Cemeteries', in *The Oxford Companion to the Garden* (Oxford/New York: Oxford University Press), pp. 101–4
Blair, Sarah, 1998, 'Cultural Geography and the Place of the Literary', *American Literary History* 10/3, pp. 544–67
Blomfield, Reginald, 1892, *The Formal Garden in England* (London: Macmillan and Co.)
Böttcher, Jakob, 2018, *Zwischen staatlichem Auftrag und gesellschaftlicher Trägerschaft: Eine Geschichte der Kriegsgräberfürsorge in Deutschland im 20. Jahrhundert (Studien zur Zivilgesellschaft*, vol. 17) (Göttingen: Vandenhoeck & Ruprecht)
Boyer, M. Christine, 1996, *The City of Collective Memory: Its Historical Imagery and Architectural Entertainments* (Cambridge, MA: The MIT Press)
Castellano, Sissi, 2000, 'Sir Edwin Lutyens e i cimiteri della Grande Guerra nel nord della Francia', *Casabella* 675 (February), pp. 6–27
Clarke, Joseph, 2007, *Commemorating the Dead in Revolutionary France: Revolution and Remembrance, 1789–1799* (Cambridge: Cambridge University Press)
Colvin, Howard, 1991, *Architecture and the After-Life* (New Haven and London: Yale University Press)
Commonwealth War Graves Commission (CWGC), offical website <http.//www.cwgc.org/>
Constant, Caroline, 1994, *The Woodland Cemetery: Towards a Spiritual Landscape* (Stockholm: Byggförlaget)
Corbin, Alain, 1982, *Le miasme et la jonquille: L'odorat et l'imaginaire social, XVIII*e*–XIX*e *siècles* (Paris: Flammarion)
Cothran, James R., and Erica Danylchak, 2018, *Grave Landscapes: The Nineteenth-Century Rural Cemetery Movement* (Columbia, SC: The University of South Carolina Press)
De Courtois, Stéphanie, Marie-Ange Maillet and Eryck de Rubercy (eds), 2018, *Esthétique du jardin paysager allemand, XVIII*e*–XIX*e *siècles* (Paris: Klincksieck)
De La Sayette, Bertrand, 1984, *Les jardins du souvenir: Cimitières militaires du Débarquement et de la bataille de Normandie, 1939–1945 = Memorial Gardens = Gärten des Gedenkens* (Condé-sur-Noireau: Éditions Charles Corlet)
De Michelis, Marco, 1981, 'The Red and the Green: Park and City in Weimar Germany', *Lotus International* 30, pp. 104–17
Destemberg, 2006, Antoine, and Benjamin Moulet, 2007, '"La mort": Mythes, rites et mémoire', *Hypothèses* 1, pp. 81–91
Duboy, Philippe, 1987, *Lequeu: Une énigme* (Paris: Hazan)
Dyer, Geoff, 1994, *The Missing of the Somme* (London: Canongate)
Ehrard Jean, 1981, *L'idée de nature en France dans la première moitié du XVIII*e *siècle* (Paris: Albin Michel)
Etlin, Richard A., 1984, *The Architecture of Death: The Transformation of the Cemetery in Eighteenth-Century Paris* (Cambridge, MA: The MIT Press)
Forty, Adrian, and Susanne Kuchler (eds), 1994, *The Art of Forgetting* (Oxford: Berg)
Foster, Jeremy, 2004, 'Creating a tenemos, positing "South Africanism": material memory, landscape practice, and the circulation of identity at Delville Wood', *Cultural Geographies* 11/3, pp. 259–90
Freud, Sigmund, 1957, 'Thoughts for the Times on War and Death' (1915), in *The Standard Edition of the Complete Psychological Works of Sigmund Freud*, 24 vols, ed. and trans. James Strachey et al. (London: Hogarth Press), vol. XIV, pp. 274–302
Freytag, Anette, 2011, and Thomas Van Driessche, 'Die Deutschen Soldatenfriedhöfe des Ersten Weltkriegs in Flandern', *Relicta: Archeologie, Monumenten- en Landschapsonderzoek in Vlaanderen 7*, pp. 163–238
Fuhrmeister, Christian, 2017, 'Robert Tischler, Chefarchitekt 1926–1959: Ein Desiderat', *RIHA Journal* 0159 (27 June) <RIHA_Journal_0159_Fuhrmeister.odt.pdf>
Fulton, Gordon, 1996, 'Roads of Remembrance', *Manitoba History* 31 <http://www.mhs.mb.ca/docs/mb_history/31/roadsofremembrance.shtml#04>
— 2018, 'Canada's Memorial Avenues of Trees: Roads of Remembrance', *Tree Avenues – From War to Peace*, international symposium, Liffol-le-Grand, Vosges, 12–13 November 2018 <https://www.allees-avenues.eu/images/R%C3%A9sum%C3%A9s_2018/10_r%C3%A9sum%C3%A9_bio_Fulton.pdf>
Geurst, Jeroen, 2010, *Cemeteries of the Great War by Sir Edwin Lutyens* (Rotterdam: 010 Publishers)
Gillis, John R. (ed.), 1994, *Commemorations: The Politics of National Identity* (Princeton, NJ: Princeton University Press)
Gothein, Marie Luise, 1979, *A History of Garden Art* (New York: Hacker Art Books; first published 1928)
Gough, Paul James, 1993, 'The Avenue of War', *Journal of the Landscape Research Group* 18/2, pp. 78–90
— 1996, 'Conifers and Commemoration: The Politics and Protocol of Planting in Military Cemeteries', *Landscape Research* 21/1, pp. 73–87
— 2018, 'The Avenue at War: From Formal Avenue to Shattered Splinters', *Tree Avenues – From War to Peace*, international symposium, Liffol-le-Grand, Vosges, 12–13 November 2018 <https://www.allees-avenues.eu/images/R%C3%A9sum%C3%A9s_2018/4_r%C3%A9sum%C3%A9_bio_Gough.pdf>
Gregory, Adrian, 1994, *The Silence of Memory, Armistice Day 1919–1946* (Oxford: Berg)
Grive-Santini, Catherine, 1999, *Guide des cimetières militaires en France* (Paris: Cherche Midi Éditeur)
Halbwachs, Maurice, 1980, *The Collective Memory*, intro. Mary Douglas, trans. F. J. Ditter Jr and V. Y. Ditter (New York: Harper Colophon); first published as *La Mémoire collective*, 1950
Hallbaum, Franz, 1932, 'Die deutsche Kriegsgräberstätte, ihr Wesen und ihre Form', *Kriegsgräberfürsorge* 10, pp. 146–51
Happe, Barbara, 1991, *Die Entwicklung der deutschen Friedhöfe von der Reformation bis 1870* (Tübingen, Tübinger Vereinigung für Volkskunde)
Hennaut, Eric, and Liliane Liesens, 2008, *Henry Lacoste: Architecte* (Paris/Brussels: AAM Éditions)
Hunt, John Dixon, and Peter Willis (eds), 1988, *The Genius of the Place: The English Landscape Garden 1620–1820* (Cambridge, MA: The MIT Press)
Iles, Jennifer, 2006, 'Recalling the Ghosts of War: Performing Tourism on the Battlefields of the Western Front', *Text and Performance Quarterly* 26/2, pp. 162–80
Jackson, Kenneth T., and Camilo José Vergara, 1989, *Silent Cities: The Evolution of the American Cemetery* (New York: Princeton Architectural Press)
*Jardins en France: 1760–1820, pays d'illusion, terre d'expériences*, 1977, exh. cat., Hôtel de Sully, Paris
*Jardins en Picardie*, 1997, training course notes, Historial de la Grande Guerre, Péronne
Jekyll, Gertrude, 1899, *Wood and Garden* (London: Longmans Green)
— 1901, *Wall and Water Gardens* (London: Country Life)
— 1908, *Colour in the Flower Garden* (London: Country Life)
Jekyll, Gertrude, and Lawrence Weaver, 1912, *Gardens for Small Country Houses* (London: Country Life)
Joiner, Sarah, 2014, 'The Evolution of the Planting Influences of the Imperial War Graves Commission from its Inception to the Modern Day', *Garden History* 42 (Autumn), pp. 90–106
Kenyon, Frederic, 1918, *War Graves. How the cemeteries abroad will be designed. Report to the Imperial War Graves Commission by Lieut.-Colonel Sir Frederic Kenyon, K.C.B., Director of the British Museum* (London: His Majesty's Stationery Office)
Kipling, Rudyard, 1925, 'The Gardener', *McCall's Magazine* (April)
— 1995, *Baa Baa, Black Sheep* (London: Penguin Books; first published 1888)
Koonz, Claudia, 1994, 'Between Memory and Oblivion: Concentration Camps in German Memory', in John R. Gillis (ed.), *Commemorations: The Politics of National Identity* (Princeton, NJ: Princeton University

Press), pp. 258–80

Kuberek, Monika, 1990, 'Die Kriegsgräberstätten des Volksbundes Deutsche Kriegsgräberfürsorge', in Michael Hütt et al., *Unglücklich das Land, das Helden nötig hat: Leiden und Sterben in den Kriegsdenkmälern des Ersten und Zweiten Weltkriegs* (Studien zur Kunst- und Kulturgeschichte, vol. 8) (Marburg: Jonas Verlag), pp. 75–90

Lambert, David, 2015, *War Memorial Parks and Gardens: Introductions to Heritage Assets* (Swindon: Historic England)

Laqueur, Thomas, 1996, 'The Past's Past' (book review), *London Review of Books* 18/18 (19 September), pp. 3–7

— 2015, *The Work of the Dead: A Cultural History of Mortal Remains* (Princeton, NJ: Princeton Unniversity Press)

Le Maner, Yves, 2018, 'L'histoire des sépultures militaires de l'Antiquité au XIXe siècle', *Chemins de Mémoire 14–18*, Centre d'Histoire et de Mémoire du Nord-Pas-de-Calais <www.cheminsdememoire-nordpasdecalais.fr/lhistoire/la-memoire-de-la-grande-guerre/lhistoire-des-sepultures-militaires-de-lantiquite-au-xixe-siecle.html>

Linden-Ward, Blanche, 1989, *Silent City on a Hill: Landscape of Memory and Boston's Mount Auburn Cemetery* (Columbus, OH: Ohio State University Press)

Longworth, Philip, 1985, *The Unending Vigil: The History of the Commonwealth War Graves Commission* (London: Leo Cooper; first published 1967)

Lowenthal, David, 1985, *The Past is a Foreign Country* (Cambridge: Cambridge University Press)

Lurz, Meinhold, 1983, '"... ein Stück Heimat in fremder Erde": Die Heldenhaine und Totenburgen des Volksbunds Deutsche Kriegsgräberfürsorge', *Arch+: Zeitschrift für Architektur und Städtebau* 71, pp. 66–70

— 1985, *Kriegerdenkmäler in Deutschland*, vol. 4., *Weimarer Republik* (Heidelberg: Esprint-Verlag)

MacDougall, Elisabeth B. (ed.), 1980, *John Claudius Loudon and the Early Nineteenth Century in Great Britain* (Washington, DC: Dumbarton Oaks Trustees for Harvard University)

Marot, Sébastien, 2003, *Sub-Urbanism and the Art of Memory* (London, AA Publications)

— 2010, *L'Art de la mémoire, le territoire et l'architecture* (Paris: La Villette)

Masson-Loodts, Isabelle, 2014, *Paysages en bataille: Les séquelles environnementales de la Grande Guerre* (Brussels, Éditions Nevicata)

Mayo, James M., 1988, *War Memorials as Political Landscape: The American Experience and Beyond* (New York: Praeger)

McKay, George, 2011, *Radical Gardening: Politics, Idealism and Rebellion in the Garden* (London: Frances Lincoln)

Monier, Olivier, 2013, 'Quand les canons se sont tus: Le traitement des corps des soldats tombés au cours de la bataille de Sarrebourg (20 août 1914)', *Revue d'Alsace* 139, pp. 291–304

Moreau (de la Sarthe), Jacques-Louis, 1778, *Essai sur les lieux et les dangers des sépultures* (Paris: P. Fr. Didot, Libraire de la Société Royale de Médecine); translated from Italian by Félix Vicq d'Azyr: *Scipione Piattoli, Saggio intorno al luogo del seppellire*, 1774

Morin, Edgar, 1951, *L'Homme et la mort* (Paris: Corréa)

Morris, Mandy S., 1997, 'Gardens "For Ever England": Landscape, Identity and the First World War British Cemeteries on the Western Front', *Ecumene* 4/4, pp. 410–34

Morrison, Toni, 1990, 'The Site of Memory', in Russell Ferguson, Martha Gever, Trinh T. Minh-ha and Cornel West (eds), *Out There: Marginalization and Contemporary Cultures* (New York/Cambridge, MA: The New Museum of Contemporary Art/The MIT Press), pp. 299–326

Mosse, George L., 1990, *Fallen Soldiers: Reshaping the Memory of the World Wars* (New York: Oxford University Press)

— 1999, *De la Grande Guerre au totalitarisme: La brutalisation des sociétés européennes* (Paris: Hachette Littératures)

Mosser, Monique, and Georges Teyssot, 1991, *Histoire des jardins de la Renaissance à nos jours* (Paris: Flammarion)

Niess, Alexandre, 2005, *Cimetières militaires et monuments aux morts de la Grande Guerre*, Direction régionale des affaires culturelles de Champagne-Ardenne-Marne

Nora, Pierre (ed.), 1992, *Les lieux de mémoire: III. Les France. I. Conflits et partages* (Paris: Gallimard)

— 1992–6, *Realms of Memory: The Construction of the French Past.* Volume 1, *Conflicts and Divisions*; Volume 2, *Traditions*; Volume 3, *Symbols* (New York: Columbia University Press)

Picard, Jean-Charles, 1987, 'L'évolution des lieux de sépulture au haut Moyen Âge', in *Liturgie et espace liturgique*, symposium, Créteil, 13–14 December 1985 (Paris: Université de Paris Val de Marne), pp. 33–48; reprinted in *Collection de l'École française de Rome*, 242 (1998), pp. 311–20

Porée, Abbé Charles Gabriel, 1749, *Lettres sur la sépulture dans les églises* (Caen: Jacques Manoury), available online at <gallica.bnf.fr/ark:/12148/bpt6k1329609>

Prost, Antoine, and Gerd Krumeich, 2015, *Verdun 1916: Une histoire franco-allemande de la bataille* (Paris: Tallandier)

Queysanne, Bruno (ed.), 2015, *L'architecture inquiétée par l'œuvre d'art: Mémorial Walter Benjamin de Dani Karava à Portbou* (Montpellier, Éditions de l'Espérou)

Racine, Michel, 1995, *Pour une politique des jardins et paysages d'intérêt culturel en région Nord-Pas-de-Calais*, intro. Philippe Nys, Préfecture de Région Nord-Pas-de-Calais/Délégation Régionale au Tourisme, Association XIX-20, ARPEJ

— 2007, *Jardins de France*, vol. 'Nord' (Paris: Ulmer)

— (ed.), 2002, *Créateurs de jardins et de paysages en France du XIXe au XXIe siècle*, vol. II (Arles: Actes Sud)

Ragon, Michel, 1981, *L'espace de la mort: Essai sur l'architecture, la décoration et l'urbanisme funéraires* (Paris: Albin Michel)

Rambert, Frank, 2014, *Jardins de guerre: Les cimetières britanniques sur le front ouest* (Geneva: MetisPresses)

Riat, Georges, *c.*1885, *L'Art des jardins* (Paris, Société française d'éditions d'art, L.-H. May)

Rietz, Simon, 2015, *Deutsche Soldatenfriedhöfe des Ersten Weltkrieges und der Weimarer Republik: Ein Beitrag zur Professionsgeschichte der Landschaftsarchitektur*, PhD dissertation, Gottfried Wilhelm Leibniz Universität, Hanover <http://edok01.tib.uni-hannover.de/edoks/e01dh15/841205302.pdf>

Robin, Ron, 1995, 'Diplomatie et commémoration: les cimetières américains en France (1918–1955)', *Revue d'Histoire moderne et contemporaine* 42/1, pp. 126–41

Scates, Bruce, 2006, *Return to Gallipoli: Walking the Battlefields of the Great War* (Cambridge: Cambridge University Press)

Sherman, Daniel J., 1994, 'Art, Commerce, and the Production of Memory in France after World War I', in John R. Gillis (ed.), *Commemorations: The Politics of National Identity* (Princeton, NJ: Princeton University Press), 1994, pp. 186–211

Thomas, Louis-Vincent, 1985, *Rites de mort, pour la paix des vivants* (Paris: Fayard)

Tison, Stéphane, 2018, 'Mourir en 14–18: De la fosse commune à la tombe individuelle' <https://www.herodote.net/Mourir_en_14_18-synthese-1961.php>

Trompette, Pascale, and Robert Howell Griffiths, 2011, 'L'économie morale de la mort au XIXe siècle: Regards croisés sur la France et l'Angleterre', *Le Mouvement social* 4/237, pp. 33–54

Turner, Paul, V., 1996, *Joseph Ramée, International Architect of the Revolutionary Era* (Cambridge: Cambridge University Press)

Urbain, Jean-Didier, 1989, *L'archipel des morts: Cimetières et mémoire en Occident* (Paris: Petite bibliothèque Payot)

Vidler, Anthony, 1983, *Claude-Nicolas Ledoux* (New York: Princeton Architectural Press)

Vovelle, Michel, 1974, *Mourir autrefois: Attitudes collectives devant la mort aux XVIIe et XVIIIe siècles* (Paris: Gallimard)

Vovelle, Michel, and Régis Bertrand, 1983, *La Ville des morts: Essai sur l'imaginaire urbain contemporain d'après les cimetières*

*provençaux* (Paris: Éditions du CNRS)
Warner, Marina, 1985, *Monument & Maidens: The Allegory of the Female Form* (London: Weidenfeld and Nicholson)
Weaver, Lawrence, 1913, *Houses and Gardens by E. L. Lutyens* (London: Country Life); reprinted by Antique Collectors' Club numerous times
Winter, Jay, 2013, *The Cambridge History of the First World War, vol. 3, Civil Society* (Cambridge: Cambridge University Press)
Wolschke-Bulmahn, Joachim, 2001, *Places of Commemoration: Search for Identity and Landscape Design* (Washington, DC: Dumbarton Oaks Trustees)
Wolschke-Bulmahn, Joachim, and Gert Groening, 1992, 'The ideology of the nature garden: Nationalistic trends in garden design in Germany during the early twentieth century', *The Journal of Garden History* 12/1, pp. 73–80
Woodbridge, Kenneth, 1971, *The Stourhead Landscape* (London: The National Trust)
Worpole, Ken, 2003, *Last Landscapes: The Architecture of the Cemetery in the West* (London, Reaktion Books)
Zadora-Rio, Elisabeth, 2000, 'Lieux d'inhumation et espaces consacrés: Le voyage du pape Urbain II en France (août 1095–août 1096)', in André Vauchez (ed.), *Lieux sacrés, Lieux de cultes, Sanctuaires: Approches terminologiques, méthodologiques, historiques et monographiques* (Rome: École française de Rome), pp. 197–213
Zilien, Johann, 1993, 'Der "Volksbund Deutsche Kriegsgräberfürsorge e.V." in der Weimarer Republik: Ein Beitrag zum politischen Denkmalkult zwischen Kaiserreich und Nationalsozialismus', *Archiv für Kulturgeschichte* 75/2 (December), pp. 445–78

This book is published with the support of

The Direction des Patrimoines, de la Mémoire et des Archives (DPMA) at the French Ministry of the Armies

The European Institute for Gardens and Landscapes and its Chairman, Didier Wirth

## ACKNOWLEDGEMENTS

The authors and the publishers would like to thank

Philippe Prost for having granted us, for this book, permission to reproduce The Ring of Remembrance, a project through which he wanted, in his own words, 'to give a shape to brotherhood and an expression to peace';

the gardeners and the staff of the

American Battle Monuments Commission

Commonwealth War Graves Commission (CWGC)

German War Graves Commission (Volksbund Deutsche Kriegsgräberfürsorge, VDK)

National Office for Veterans and Victims of War (ONACVG)

Service pour l'Entretien des Sépultures militaires allemandes (SESMA)

for the admirable maintenance of the war graves and memorials of both world wars;

The Association of Landscapes and Memorials of the Great War;

Le Souvenir français;

Stéphanie de Courtois, historian, teacher-researcher at ENSAV (Versailles);

Laurence Garfield, landscape designer;

Frédérique Lorenzi, Parks and Gardens PACA;

Peter Paessler, Volksbund Deutsche Kriegsgräberfürsorge (VDK);

Béatrice Saurel, landscape artist;

Veterans Affairs Canada / Anciens Combattants Canada;

The War Heritage Institute.

## COLOPHON

*Publisher:*
Mercatorfonds (director: Bernard Steyaert)

*Editor:*
Michel Racine

*Editorial coordination and picture research:*
Marianne Thys, Alice d'Ursel

*Translation:*
Paula Cook

*Graphic design and typesetting:*
Grégoire Romefort

*Repro, printing and binding:*
Graphius
*Printed on* Luxo Art Samt 150 gr/m$^2$

Copyright © for the texts: the authors
Copyright © photographs Christine Bastin and Jacques Evrard
© Bastin & Evrard-SOFAM/ADAGP

Distributed in Belgium, the Netherlands and Luxembourg by Exhibitions International, Leuven
www.mercatorfonds.be
ISBN 978-94-6230-120-7
D/2019/703/21

Distributed outside Belgium, the Netherlands and Luxembourg by Yale University Press, New Haven and London
yalebooks.com/art – yalebooks.co.uk
ISBN YALE 978-0-300-24649-0
Library of Congress Control Number: 2019941043

All rights reserved. No part of this publication may be reproduced or transmitted in any form or by any means, electronic or mechanical, including photocopy, recording or any other information storage and retrieval system without prior permission in writing from the publisher.

## PHOTOGRAPHIC CREDITS

We have endeavoured to enforce legal copyright requirements, but were not always able to trace the origin of some images. Anyone who considers themselves entitled to assert such rights is asked to contact the publisher.

Christine Bastin & Jacques Evrard: front and back covers, frontispiece, pp. 2, 4, 7, 8, 14 right, 19 left, 21, 27 right, 28, 33, 45, 46 right, 48–225

Alamy Stock Photo: pp. 11 left (Angelo Hornak), right (Barbara Opitz), 12 bottom right (LianeM), 19 right, 20 right (Eric Nathan)
American Battle Monuments Commission: p. 38 left & right
ANTEA-Archéologie: p. 9
DPMA Archives: pp. 34, 35 right, 36
John Armagh: p. 16 bottom right
Berkeley, Gertrude Jekyll Collection, Environmental Design Archives, UC Berkeley: p. 22 left & right
Bernard Klein collection: p. 27 bottom centre
Simon Rietz collection: pp. 26, 27 top & bottom left, 31 left
Stéphanie de Courtois: p. 12 left & top right
Edwardx: p. 17 left
Fin Fahey: p. 16 top right
Paul Gough: pp. 42, 43
Hobart, State Library and Archive Service | Tasmania Libraries: p. 39 left
© Junko Kimura/Jana/ZUMApress.com: p. 46 left
London, The British Museum: p. 15 top
Isabelle Loodts: p. 46 left
Frédérique Lorenzi: p. 37
New Haven, Yale University Library: p. 16 left
Ozankk: p. 11 centre
Paris, National Library of France, Prints and Photography departments: pp. 13, 14 top
Guillaume Pichard: p. 35 left
Michel Racine: pp. 5, 20 left, 23
Christa Reichardt: p. 25
© Roger-Viollet/Photonews: p. 14 bottom left
Béatrice Saurel: pp. 15 centre & bottom, 47 top
Lars Soltek: p. 24
Squared: p. 46 bottom right
Myriam Thyes: p. 10
© TREENET: p. 39 top & bottom right
Courtesy Veterans Affairs Canada/Anciens Combattants Canada: p. 41
Washington, DC, Library of Congress, Prints and Photographs Division: pp. 18
Other sources: Günter Kaufmann (ed.), *Langemarck: Das Opfer der Jugend an allen Fronten*, Stuttgart, 1938: pp. 29, 30, 31 right
Winfried Nerdinger and Ekkehard Mai, *Wilhelm Kreis: Architekt zwischen Kaiserreich und Demokratie* 1873–1955, Munich/Berlin, 1994: p. 32 left
Ernst May, 'Krieger-Friedhöfe: einer Division an der rumänischen Sereth-Front', *Deutsche Kunst und Dekoration*, 1917, pp. 216–22 (p. 218): p. 32 right

Cover: The Ring of Remembrance, Ablain-Saint-Nazaire French War Cemetery, Pas-de-Calais, WW1 (architect: Philippe Prost)

End papers: Neuve-Chapelle Indian Memorial, Richebourg, Pas-de-Calais, WW1 (architect: Herbert Baker)

Back cover: Villers-Bretonneux British War Cemetery and Australian National Memorial, Somme, WW1 (architects: Edwin Lutyens and George H. Goldsmith)

Neuville-en-Condroz 'Ardennes American Cemetery', Neupré, Liège, Belgium, WW2 (architects: Reinhard, Hofmeister & Walquist; sculptor: Carl Paul Jennewein)